PRINCE DUSTIN
AND
CLARA

LEGENDS OF THE BLACK FOREST
BOOK THREE

D0898433

PRINCE DUSTIN
AND
CLARA

LEGENDS OF THE BLACK FOREST
BOOK THREE

DANIEL LEE NICHOLSON

by

Fossil Mountain Publishing, LLC

FOSSIL
MOUNTAIN PUBLISHING

ACKNOWLEDGEMENTS

Fossil Mountain Publishing would like to thank the dance, performing, and visual arts communities for their commitment to providing excellence in instruction and their devotion to inspiring our youth.

"There is no limit to what a person can do that has been inspired by *The Arts*!"

Printed in the United States of America

First Edition / Hardcover

Foreword by Silvino da Silva,
The Ruth Page Center for the Arts

ISBN-13: 978-0-9986191-7-0 (Paperback)
ISBN-13: 978-0-9986191-8-7 (Hardcover)

Library of Congress Control Number: 2021935729

Fossil Mountain Publishing, LLC
PO BOX 48092
Watauga, TX 76148
Dallas - Fort Worth | Texas

www.FossilMountainPublishing.com

for

Lee Morris Reed, Junior

and in homage to the original creators of
"The Nutcracker":

E.T.A. Hoffmann
Alexandre Dumas
Pyotr Ilyich Tchaikovsky
Marius Petipa
Lev Ivanov

TABLE OF CONTENTS

FOREWORD

SILVINO DA SILVA
THE RUTH PAGE CENTER FOR THE ARTS

PROLOGUE

MERLIN'S MAGICAL STONES

ACT ONE

1   THE TROLLS AND SERIHILDA / 1
2   CLARA STAHLBAUM / 15
3   LACHE LAKE MONSTERS / 29
4   THE ICE PALACE / 39
5   CREATURES EVERYWHERE / 47
6   KING DUSTIN OF KONFETENBURG / 57
7   THE TORNADO / 67
8   BEFORE THE FULL MOON RISES / 71

ACT TWO

9   THE ENCHANTED BLACK FOREST / 79
10   THE ENCHANTRESS / 87
11   LAND OF THE TREE FAIRIES / 93
12   GONE! SHE VANISHED! / 99
13   FALLING / 109
14   MARCH OF THE TROLLS / 117
15   MOZART GOES MAD / 127

16   THE SWAMPLAND / 135
17   THE THING IN THE SWAMP / 143
18   THE PLAN / 147
19   CHAMBER OF HORROR / 155
20   CAVE CREATURES / 165
21   LAND OF ZAUBERIN / 173

ACT THREE

22   ENCHANTED ZAUBERIN CASTLE / 185
23   THE BEAST / 193
24   BEAUTY / 201
25   THE TRANSFORMATION / 209
26   FULL MOON RISING / 215
27   GRAND FINALE / 233
28   ADVENTURES DEEP IN THE BLACK / 245
       FOREST

❖ ❖ ❖

ACCOLADES
DISCUSSION AND NOTES
ABOUT US

FOREWORD

Creativity takes courage. So, imagine the courage it took to create an original idea that not only captures the magic of a well-loved and iconic holiday story, but also takes readers on new and amazing quests with familiar characters. The "Prince Dustin and Clara" children's book series by Daniel Lee Nicholson is a re-imagining of "The Nutcracker" story, and with the publication of this third and final installment, a genius idea comes to a satisfying and enthralling conclusion. What an adventure!

I have a quote that I like to refer to by Vladimir Nabokov that says: *"There is, it would seem, in the dimensional scale of the world a kind of delicate meeting place between imagination and knowledge, a point, arrived at by diminishing large things and enlarging small ones that is intrinsically artistic."* In this delicate balance, I believe great art, great ideas can be born.

But to have great art and great ideas, the arts must be nurtured. Children must be allowed to create, play and dream to their heart's desire. A framework that allows for unfettered dreaming and creating is not open to every child, however. There is a great deficit in the access to quality, transformative arts education, especially for those children that are economically disadvantaged or marginalized. Children from every culture, geographic region and socioeconomic level deserve quality arts learning. Closing the achievement gap cannot happen without commitment, resources and dedication to bettering the lives of at-risk children.

The Ruth Page Center for the Arts and its School of Dance celebrate 50-years as a non-profit performing arts organization in 2021. Our mission to be a platform for developing great artists and connecting them with audiences and community, is the driving force that propels us forward and informs our programs. As with all organizations, there are moments when one wonders if our hard work and commitment has had the positive impact we strive for. For me, the answer to this question came quite unexpectedly on a cold winter's morning in an email.

I was told in that email "The Ruth Page School of Dance changed my life!" The correspondent of the email came through our Young Dancers Training Program, performed in the annual "Nutcracker" concerts and eventually became a professional dancer. Traveling to and from Chicago's south side for dance training was sometimes a hardship, and the family was not one of means, but our young dancer had parents who felt that arts education was important. The skills learned in the studio and on stage go well beyond just remembering steps. Dance training engages a child's brain, body and emotions in different ways, encouraging confidence and self-expression.

Every day, the arts help children transform, positively impacting their future. It helps them to dream beyond any physical confines and connects them with the world. And, the arts helped one talented dancer to transform into a great writer, meeting at the intersection of knowledge and imagination, and creating entirely new dreams and adventures.

To everyone who supports the arts, for everyone who lifts a child's voice – **Thank you!**

Silvino da Silva
Acting Executive Director
The Ruth Page Center for the Arts
April 15, 2021

LEGENDS OF THE BLACK FOREST
BOOK THREE

Prologue

Merlin's Magical Stones

***It was a hazy, humid day many, many years
ago***. In a magical land of fairies and sorcerers,
a stone castle stood tall on the horizon.
Magnificent evergreens surrounded the
castle, touching the sky in every direction.

Majestic mountains draped this
magical land. They looked as though they
were added by the stroke of a brush serving as
background to the castle. Each mountaintop
was higher than the last until they reached
the heavens above. White velvet snow capped
the tops of each peak like a sprinkling of
marshmallows on hot chocolate.

A soaring tower flanked the side of the
castle. Mysterious dark shadows swirled and
twirled around the stone structure. The
shadows spun and spun and spun. Around and
around and around, they flew like a carousel

of flying wooden horses on a merry-go-round. It could have been a place of fun and amusement—*had this castle been anywhere else.*

However, this castle was not just anywhere. Nor was this just any other castle. This was Niedertrachtig Castle, in the realm of the Dark Forces, Deeper in the Black Forest. Guests never traveled to Niedertrachtig Castle—*not the sort that was living, anyway.*

A century earlier, a good and fair sorcerer, Wizard Herr Drosselmeyer, cast a powerful spell against the Dark Forces. The curse included his evil twin brother, Wizard Drachenmeyer. The incantation prevented the Dark Forces from being able to travel to the other lands in the forest.

The people, animals, and creatures that lived in the Land of Sweets and Land of Snow rejoiced. They were safe from the Dark Forces forever, *so everyone thought.*

❖ ❖ ❖

One-hundred years passed. Wicked Wizard Drachenmeyer learned of three magical stones. The stones had been buried many, many years ago by Merlin, a very powerful wizard. Merlin hid the magical stones to ensure that they would never be used against him.

After learning about the stones, Drachenmeyer used sorcery to discover their locations. He then retrieved them from their hidden places.

Drachenmeyer had planned to use the magical stones to capture his brother, the good wizard, Drosselmeyer. He sought revenge on his brother for casting the spell against him and the Dark Forces a century earlier.

However, plans do not always go as planned.

In the end, it was the wicked Wizard Drachenmeyer that was captured and imprisoned by Herr Drosselmeyer. The evil wizard was trapped in the tower at Niedertrachtig Castle.

And there he will remain, for all of eternity—*so the legend goes.*

End of Prologue

"By the way, my name is Serihilda."

ACT 1

-1-

The Trolls and Serihilda

Part One

Deeper in the Black Forest, far away from the Land of Sweets and Land of Snow, evil lurks in every shadow. Far away from sugar plums and candy canes, gingerbread, and apple strudel, eerie creatures roam and wander.

Scary monsters, sorcerers, wild animals, and giant beasts dwell in this forsaken place. The land is full of enchantment and magic but seldom a happy ending.

A band of wicked trolls also live in this perilous land. Trolls are gruesome creatures that fear nothing. They have big heads, enormous ears, and very large feet.

Trolls inhabit the dark and dreadful caves of Mount Gruslig. As vicious as wolves, Trolls roam the woods in packs, searching for their next victim to crush or prey to squash. With one stomp of their foot, they have taken down many giants and slaughtered many beasts. They then eat their meal by the campfire—singing, laughing, and filling their bellies late into the night until they pass out.

Although dwarfish in stature, trolls are powerful and quite strong. Their necks are so thick with muscle that their deep voices frighten small animals when they speak.

Trolls are hideous creatures with hairy bodies, bulging eyes, and club-shaped noses. They seem to prefer the smell of rot and decay. They never bother to discard the bones of a half-eaten victim but simply toss the remnants into a pile.

They attack in the twilight of the night before their victims ever have a chance to open their eyes to the nightmare. Trolls have no purpose in their slaughters other than to slay every being that crosses their path or trespasses onto their land.

Serihilda, the lady that lives at Zauberin Castle, will be their next victim.

❖ ❖ ❖

"Do you have any questions about your orders?" The Commander of the Trolls said. His deep voice echoed off the walls of the cave like the clap of thunder.

"Sir, your orders were clear," the lead troll replied. He then shot a glance at the other troll.

"No questions, Sir," the second troll remarked, avoiding eye contact with the Commander. Although he stood as straight as he could, his back was still slightly hunched.

The Commander continued, "Serihilda must be handled tonight." His voice was monotone, utterly void of any emotion. And his black eyes looked like pools of darkness on his huge head.

"We will take care of her before the sun rises," the lead troll responded.

"Do you know the consequences if you are not successful?" The Commander glared at the trolls—one then the other.

The lead troll replied with confidence, "Your orders will be carried out. We will make it back by dawn, Sir."

The second troll looked down, appearing deep in thought. "Yes, Commander, we know the consequences."

The Commander sniffed hard. Green ooze that had dripped down his face from his nostrils was sucked back up into his nose. The Commander then spat the green glob out of his mouth onto the ground.

SPLAT!

With a dismissal wave of his hand, the Commander of the Trolls turned and walked away. Both trolls listened to the sound of the Commander's heavy footsteps.

"We must depart now." The eyes of the lead troll glimmered. The second troll looked askance. He did not appear to share the same enthusiasm.

❖ ❖ ❖

Part Two

The lady, Serihilda, lives in a castle Deeper in the Black Forest in the Land of Zauberin.

Zauberin Castle sits high on a hill. Tall evergreen trees surround the castle's outer perimeter. The castle's structure is very grand, with turrets and towers. Ivy and pink roses climb up the sides of the stone walls, softening the formal facade.

A babbling brook flows around the castle, ending somewhere in the woods. The water in the brook sparkles effervescent green. Bubbles float into the air just above the water like a frothy bubble bath.

A colossal stone fountain is set in the center of the courtyard of the castle. At night, the water sounds musical, like a lullaby.

A strange-looking beast serves as the centerpiece of the fountain. The stone beast has the head of a predator animal, a lion's body, and a dragon's wings. It resembles a gargoyle, except for the head. Gargoyles are quite prominent on roofs of castles. Many believe they frighten away evil spirits.

Everywhere in the garden, beautiful flowers can be seen. Flower beds filled with marigolds, daisies, violets, and morning glory pop with vibrant color. Pink delicate peonies, yellow daffodils, and stalks of lavender are plentiful. The fragrant blend of the flowers smells magical.

The courtyard of Zauberin Castle is truly delightful.

❖ ❖ ❖

The two trolls left the caves of Mount Gruslig earlier in the day. The moon and stars were now glowing brightly in the dark-blue velvet sky. The trolls peered into the courtyard of Zauberin Castle until well after midnight.

"They should be sleep by now," the lead troll said, looking up at one of the windows. "Even Krieger," he continued.

The second troll nodded.

"After we crush Serihilda, let's get Krieger," The lead troll said as he pounded his foot into the ground. The ground sunk several inches, leaving a deep imprint. No matter how hard the trolls pounded their feet, their bones never broke.

"Hermann, that wasn't part of our orders. We were instructed only to take care of Serihilda, not Krieger," the second troll said to the lead troll.

"Georg," the lead troll responded, "do I have to do all the thinking for both of us?"

The lead troll continued, "If we do away with Serihilda, then we will have to worry about Krieger."

Georg paused for a moment and then replied, "Hmm, you make a good point, I guess." Although Georg understood the logic, he hung his head.

"Trust me. The Commander will grant us special privileges when he finds out that we got rid of Krieger, too," Hermann said.

After some thought, Georg reluctantly nodded in agreement.

The trolls then started across the courtyard. Even though trolls have large feet and only four toes, they are quite agile beings. For beasts, not even four feet tall, they move quite swiftly.

Hermann and Georg stopped and looked at the large fountain in the center of the courtyard. The moon caught a glimpse of their stumpy silhouettes as the trolls stood still.

Their hairy bodies made the trolls look like wild animals. Trolls had faces that looked human, *in a hideous sort of way*. Under the glow of the moon, Hermann and Georg looked half-human and half-beast.

The trolls continued around the courtyard to a side door in the lower part of the castle. Hermann raised his foot to pound the door. Georg held tight to the door's lever to keep the door from slamming on the ground. With one kick, the trolls were inside the dungeon.

Hermann wriggled his fat toes. "Remind me to soak my feet in that fountain when we leave."

"There's not enough room in that fountain for your big feet," Georg chuckled, being careful not to laugh too loudly.

"Humph," Hermann grunted.

The trolls stepped over the door jamb and cocked their heads, listening for movement. Not even a mouse stirred. Like most creatures Deep in the Black Forest, trolls could see in the dark. Hermann and Georg scanned the dungeon.

Adjacent to a long corridor was a set of stairs that led up to the main floor of Zauberin Castle. A large wooden door hung at the top of the staircase. The trolls walked up the stairs, being careful not to make any excessive noise.

Reaching the top of the staircase, Hermann said, "It's open." With a click, they were inside the castle. The door opened to a short passageway that led to the Great Hall.

The Great Hall was grand and spacious. It was large enough to accommodate many guests for dining and dancing. The room had enormously high ceilings, making the trolls look even shorter.

"Serihilda's bed-chamber should be one floor up, at the end of the hall," Hermann said.

Georg nodded stiffly.

"When we get to her chamber, we must be quick." Hermann proceeded to the center staircase that led to the upper chambers. "The Commander had said that her sleeping quarters would be to the left side of the staircase."

Georg again nodded. Fear could be seen in his eyes, which was unusual for a troll. It was assumed that *all* trolls were fearless and would face any danger. Maybe Georg was an exception. He kept looking around, possibly looking for Krieger.

Green heavy drapery with gold cords covered all the windows. The hall was furnished with velvet sofas and chairs in the same shade of green. Although gold sconces were mounted to the walls, the castle was gravely dark. None of the sconces were lit.

Hermann and Georg ambled up the center staircase. They tip-toed as best they could with their large feet. Despite their best efforts, the stairs creaked with each step.

Georg continued to look around. Beads of sweat were now trickling down his forehead.

When Hermann reached the top of the staircase, he waved for Georg to hurry. He then proceeded down the corridor toward Serihilda's bed-chamber.

Georg looked around nervously as he walked down the hallway. All the doors to the rooms were quite tall—possibly four or five times the trolls' height. Georg gulped as he looked up at the height of the doors.

Hermann was further down the hall. His eyes glistened, and his mouth drooled as he approached Serihilda's chamber.

Hermann glowed with anticipation. Trolls enjoyed crushing their victims. Serihilda would be no exception.

Hermann waited for Georg before entering Serihilda's bed-chamber.

When Georg reached the lead troll, sweat was pouring down his forehead like rain. Fear shone all over his face.

Hermann stared at Georg and shook his head, apparently disgusted by the troll's fear. Hermann then turned around and twisted the doorknob of Serihilda's bed-chamber.

Georg followed behind, visibly shaking. The hair on his body looked like it was magnetized. It stuck straight out.

Serihilda's bedroom was decorated similarly to the rest of the castle, with one exception. Beautiful flowers in every shade of the rainbow graced vases and were planted in clay pots. Flowers were everywhere in the chamber, scenting the air.

Heavy curtains hung on the windows blocking the moonlight. A big four-poster bed rested on the opposite wall. Vines of ivy grew up the bedposts.

The chamber looked like a secret garden—*to anyone that could see in the dark.* To everyone else, the room looked like a black hole.

The trolls stepped slowly toward Serihilda's bed. While Hermann gleamed with glee, Georg trembled like a cornered porcupine.

The plan was for Georg to pull back the bedsheets. Hermann would then use his big foot and crush Serihilda—*then no more Serihilda.*

Hermann's eyes glowed. He signaled for Georg to pull back the bedsheets.

Georg nodded. He then slowly pulled back the green satin sheets. His hands trembled. Inch-by-inch, Georg slowly pulled back the bed linen.

Serihilda did not move.

Hermann smiled as he moved even closer. He then lifted his right foot. He was ready. His face glistened, and his eyes bulged. They looked like they were about to pop out of their sockets.

Serihilda appeared to be sound asleep. She still did not move. Like most of the trolls' victims, Serihilda would be asleep through the nightmare.

A single bead of sweat dripped off the tip of Georg's nose onto the green bed sheet.

PLOP!

Both Hermann and Georg stared at the wet, dark spot created by the drop of sweat. *Then—*

SWOOSH! SWOOSH!

It was quick. Hermann and Georg had no time to run. An enormous beast with piercing purple eyes swooped down from the ceiling.

The creature had enormous wings, like a dragon. Its face resembled that of a predator animal, and its body looked like that of a lion.

The monstrous creature was massive. It captured the trolls between its enormous wings. The monster's claws glistened like knives. Nothing could escape their grip without being shredded to pieces.

In one swoop, the creature's wings fully engulfed both trolls.

As the beast closed its wings, a fresh lavender scent filled the bed-chamber. The scent was so strong that it choked the air.

An eerie cackle erupted from the beast as it squeezed its wings even tighter. The windows in the room shook.

Just then, the door of the room flung open and slammed against the adjacent wall. A vast shadow, almost as tall as the doorway, stood just inside the bed-chamber.

"Sorceress?" the large shadow said in a low voice.

The Sorceress, Lady Serihilda, continued to laugh. Her massive wings glowed an iridescent color, matching her purple eyes.

The Sorceress, in beast form, then opened her wings. The trolls were gone. Sparkly purple dust floated into the air. Within moments, the dust danced away.

Krieger, the Ogre, watched as Serihilda turned back into her lovely human form.

Serihilda's long black and white hair draped down her back, dusting the floor. Her eyes were the deepest shade of purple. Serihilda's face held the innocence of a debutante.

Serihilda gazed at her bed. She was never underneath the bedsheets. Her covers were floating inches above her bed, taking the form of her body.

Sorceress Serihilda, the lady of Zauberin Castle, would not be the trolls' next victim.

❖ ❖ ❖

Hermann and Georg did not make it back to the caves of Mount Gruslig. At dawn, the Commander of the Trolls stared in the direction of Zauberin Castle. He recounted his final words to the two trolls:

"Do you know the consequences if you are not successful?"

❖ ❖ ❖

Part Three

The next morning, when Sorceress Serihilda awakened, she declared to Krieger, the Ogre, "I will rule the Dark Forces and all the Black Forest. Never again will the Dark Forces be suppressed. NEVER!"

"It has been a hundred years. A century has passed. With the passage of time, changes would be inevitable," the Ogre reflected. The Ogre was very intelligent. The Sorceress relied upon him for counsel.

"I will make Drosselmeyer suffer for his actions. They will all suffer!"

"Yes, Sorceress," Krieger said.

Serihilda continued, "I will pay a visit to the other realm deep in the Black Forest."

Krieger nodded. "They say that the King of Konfetenburg and the Snow Queen have joined forces and rule the lands there. They are good friends with Wizard Drossel–"

"Wait, did you say King of Konfetenburg?" the Sorceress started. "But, what about–"

Krieger interrupted, "King Marc's son now rules over the Land of Sweets, the Kingdom of Konfetenburg."

A smell from the lower floor caught Sorceress Serihilda's immediate attention. Serihilda turned her head, holding her nose. "What is that horrible smell?"

Krieger responded, "Druella is cooking breakfast."

"Breakfast?" Serihilda said in a bewildered tone. "After all these years, she still doesn't know how to cook!" Serihilda threw her hands up in the air.

Krieger rubbed the side of his face. "She tries," the Ogre responded in an empathetic tone. "Are you ready to go down for breakfast, Sorceress?"

"Let me water the flowers first." Sorceress Serihilda then snapped her fingers. Sparkly purple dust floated from her fingertips into the air. Water then flowed from the ceiling, directly above each pot of flowers, watering them.

Krieger waited at the bed-chamber door for the Sorceress.

Sorceress Serihilda shook her head as she and the Ogre headed for breakfast. "Whoever told Druella that *eye of newt* tastes good in porridge was sadly mistaken."

-2-

Clara Stahlbaum

It was early in the afternoon—a perfect time to hang out at Lache Lake in the Black Forest.

The wind gently blew the branches and flowers while the earthy scent of musk filtered the air. Birds, perched on tree limbs, tweeted and chirped. It was the kind of day that attracted all sorts of animals *and creatures*.

The sun was no longer beaming down with its intense heat, and the water's temperature was a comfortable eighty-three degrees. The boy campers had made their way to the lake for a day of swimming.

The heads of boys bobbed against the surface of the water as they swam. One boy stood with binoculars on a small platform on the shore, watching the others.

Boys not swimming, played on the beach. The rippling water softened their excited voices. Summer camp had officially begun at Lache Lake.

Camp Lache Lake was the only summer program of its kind. Kids would come from near and far to attend. Years earlier, the camp only admitted boys. However, within a few years of its opening, the camp was open to girls.

❖ ❖ ❖

Every summer, Clara Stahlbaum and her younger brother, Fritz, attended Camp Lache Lake.

Clara was always excited to go to camp. She and her friends thought of it as a big pajama party. Clara and her best friend, Marie, enjoyed doing arts and crafts, hanging out, and dancing. Both girls always performed in the dance show at the end of camp. Dancing was their favorite thing to do.

The only thing Clara did not like about camp was that Fritz, and his troublesome friends, attended camp at the same time. However, since her journeys Deep in the Black Forest, things that Fritz would do that would typically annoy Clara did not bother her as much anymore.

Although braver than she was when she first traveled deeper into the forest, Clara still shivered, remembering the eerie encounters. Nobody believed in wizards or magic in Clara's hometown, so Clara never told anyone about her journeys, not even Marie. The *Secrets of the Black Forest* remained Clara's secret.

❖ ❖ ❖

"Hi, Rupert!" Clara and Marie spoke at the same time, entering the Dance Hall at Camp Lache Lake.

"Hello," Rupert responded. "Are both of you auditioning for Lead this summer?"

"Yes. Even though I won't turn fourteen until later in the year, Miss Patti allowed me to audition," Clara responded. Both Rupert and Marie smiled, hearing Clara's remark. The friends always supported each other.

Mirrors lined the walls of the Dance Hall. Clara's chestnut brown hair was pinned in a low bun. A tint of green was on the lids of her large brown eyes. Her rosy lips shined with gloss.

Clara was dressed similarly to the other girls. In dance class, all the girls wore short-sleeved dirndls. The white tops were fitted, and the skirts were made of striped black and beige muslin. Loose calico pantaloons were worn underneath. The skirts brushed their knees as the girls stretched and warmed up.

Rupert wore a white shirt and vest with breeches that came halfway down his leg. It did not appear to bother him that he was the only boy at the audition. Perhaps he was used to being the only boy in dance class.

Many of the girls waved to Clara and Marie. Some girls whispered, watching them warm up. It was known that both Clara and Marie were amongst the best dancers at the Dance Academy.

The other girls tried to mimic their dance movements. Clara always smiled. Sometimes she would show the other girls how to do a technique.

Clapping her hands twice for attention, Miss Patti announced, "Everyone, the auditions are about to begin. Please get your numbers and take your places."

Although Miss Patti had a stern look, her deep-set eyes conveyed warmth. Her elongated neck and graceful arms displayed the elegance of a former prima ballerina.

Hearing Miss Patti's voice, the dance hall immediately went silent. Only the shushing of excited feet could be heard as the dancers rushed to the table to get their numbers.

The auditions for Round One were about to begin.

❖ ❖ ❖

The boy campers, all but Rupert, were spending the day at the lake. While the older boys swam, Fritz and the younger boys played games on the shore.

Fritz, nearly nine, was considered one of the older, younger boys. Fritz was always laughing, smiling, and having fun. The other young boys liked hanging around Fritz. Because Fritz liked to play pranks, the young boys usually got into trouble for one reason or another.

Fritz turned and said to the other boys on the shore, "I can make a rock skip five times."

One boy replied, "I can beat that."

A second boy boasted, "I had a rock skip ten times last summer."

"Ten times?" Fritz said, doubtful.

"Wanna see?" the boy offered.

Fritz stood tall and challenged both boys. "Let's see who can make a rock skip the most."

"Okay," the boys responded in unison, giving each other a side glance.

Fritz added, "And whoever wins gets to have the losers' dessert for the rest of camp."

The boy who claimed he could beat Fritz gulped.

The second boy, who claimed he had a rock skip ten times, said, "It's on! That's a triple-scoop of ice cream for me every night."

"First, you have to win," Fritz added as he looked for a rock.

After a few minutes, Fritz seemed pleased with a rock he picked. He practiced flinging his wrist. The other two boys did the same.

"DO THAT SOMEWHERE ELSE!" one of the older boys yelled, obviously not wanting to get whacked in the head by a flying rock.

Fritz pointed. "Let's go over there." All the younger boys followed Fritz.

Reaching the designated area, the three boys lined up at the edge of the lake. Bruno, Fritz's close friend, volunteered to count off.

"Get-on-your-mark," Bruno said, raising his right arm.

Fritz stared at the lake with intense eyes. He held his rock between his fingers, with his wrist tilted.

"Get ready," Bruno continued.

Fritz angled his rock and narrowed his eyes.

"Go!" Bruno yelled at the top of his lungs.

Fritz stooped low and flicked his wrist, flinging his rock into the lake. The other two boys followed.

PLOP!

The boy that said that he could beat Fritz lowered his eyes. His big round rock sank to the bottom of the lake without skipping even once.

"One, two, three," Fritz yelled, watching his rock skip. "Keep going," Fritz pleaded. All eyes were on the lake.

After a moment, Fritz's eyes dropped. His rock sank after skipping only four times.

"Drats!" Fritz bellowed.

"I won! I won!" The second boy jumped up and down. His rock skipped the lake five times before sinking.

Fritz challenged, "You said you could make a rock skip ten times. That was only five."

"But I still beat both of you."

Fritz shrugged, acknowledging his defeat. He then looked back at the water as if hoping his rock would re-surface.

"What's that?" Fritz exclaimed, pointing at something plopping about in the lake.

Fritz squinted his eyes. "Are those Frogs?"

❖ ❖ ❖

Kröte, the Toad, splashed about in the water. The frogs ventured down to Lache Lake for the cooler temperatures.

Kröte and his toad friends lived on the river deeper in the Black Forest. They were not ordinary frogs. They were not like the frogs at Lache Lake.

Kröte, like most animals, Deep in the Black Forest, could understand and even talk with human animals—*human animals that could speak with animals, that is.*

Centuries ago, the animals and humans that lived Deep in the Black Forest learned to communicate with each other without either group having to change their language. That's how things were in the enchanted lands of the Black Forest.

"The boys are back this summer," Kröte said, full of excitement. All the frogs leaped with joy and expressed their excitement.

"We had fun playing with them last year!" one of the toads exclaimed.

"Remember, we leaped and splashed water all over them."

"They liked it! They said something about feeling like they were swimming under a waterfall."

"They didn't want to leave the lake."

"I had a lot of fun jumping and splashing in the water!"

"Me too."

"Let's swim closer to the shore. Maybe the boys will play with us again." Kröte smiled, kicking his hind legs behind his plump body. The frog's jewel-like eyes blinked on each side of his face.

Dragonflies were everywhere, skimming the lake. One of the dragonflies flew close to Kröte. Kröte flicked his long tongue–the dragonfly was gone.

"Yummy!" Kröte said, digesting his snack. He then belched loudly.

"Follow me." Kröte waved to the other toads as he swam toward the shore.

The toads swam closer and closer to the boys. Their brownish-gray skin gleamed like metal under the fading sun as they splashed in the water.

The toads jumped and leaped, trying to get the boys' attention. Water splished and splashed. It sounded like the pitter-patter of rain boots through puddles on a rainy day.

Splish-splash!   ***Splish-splash!***

❖ ❖ ❖

"They **are** frogs!" Fritz exclaimed.

Bruno and the other boys nodded. Their eyes sparkled as they gazed at the frogs splashing toward them.

"Let's get in!" Fritz shouted. The boys pulled off their shoes and shirts and jumped in the lake in their knee-length lederhosen trousers. They pulled down the suspenders so that they could swim freely.

The young boys swam closer toward the toads, and the toads swam closer toward the boys. One would have thought that the toads and boys were old friends meeting up.

"This is just like last summer!" Fritz yelled, recalling how they had played in the lake with frogs the summer prior.

"Yeah! I remember," Bruno responded.

The toads and boys reached each other just a short distance from the shore. The toads seemed to know that the higher they leaped, the bigger the splash.

Kröte leaped ten feet into the air before diving into the water.

SPLISH-SPLASH!

Water splashed all over Fritz and Bruno, lashing their faces. Except for their wide grins, the boys looked like they had been crying.

"That was a good one!" Fritz screamed. Bruno jumped with joy. The boys' hair was soaked and soggy.

Three toads jumped high in the air and slammed their bodies into the lake. Water showered the boys.

"Ahhh!" Fritz exclaimed as he dived underneath the water.

Fritz was amazed at the colorful fish and animals that he saw that lived in the lake. While underwater, Fritz waved his hand, trying to play with the fish. Brightly-colored rainbow trout quickly swam away, avoiding Fritz's touch. Tiny bubbles escaped from their mouths. Unlike the toads, the trout did not want to play.

Kröte, however, wanted to play. He swam under the water toward Fritz and seemed to blow air into his cheeks, puffing them up.

Fritz looked at Kröte with wide eyes, obviously in awe at the frog's funny face and balloon cheeks.

Kröte then opened and closed his mouth, speaking. The toad must have forgotten that these boys were not from lands Deep in the Black Forest. These boys did not know how to talk with animals. Kröte continued to puff his cheeks, holding a one-sided conversation.

Fritz looked at the scores of toads as they plunged all around him under the water. Fritz then re-surfaced for air. He had held his breath as long as he could.

The frogs leaped and dived, splattering the boys.

Water splashed in big droplets spraying Fritz and the other boys. The boys screamed with excitement.

As the toads jumped higher, the boys screamed even louder.

Eventually, the older boys swam over and joined in on the fun. The toads, possibly delighted by the larger audience, jumped higher and higher, plunging deeper and deeper into the water. The frogs created a titanic splash each time.

S-P-L-A-S-H!   *S-P-L-A-S-H!*

After a couple of hours, the sun began to set. The boy that remained on shore, holding the binoculars, yelled. "It's getting late, everyone. Please come out of the water and return to the campgrounds." None of the boys moved toward the shore.

"It's getting late. Everyone has to come out of the water." The boy looked through his binoculars, then added more forcefully than before, "Now!"

The older boys began to swim toward the shore. Fritz and the younger boys waded toward the shore slowly.

After a moment, Fritz's eyes lit up. "Let's take the frogs back to the cabins. It'll be fun."

"Yeah, we can play a game to see whose frog can leap the farthest," one of the boys replied

"Maybe," Fritz said. "Everybody, grab a frog."

Fritz's eyes gleamed as he rubbed his chin. All the boys then looked in the water for a frog to take back to their cabins.

Bruno said, dipping his hand into the water, "I am going to look for one with a lot of warts. They are older and bigger and probably can leap the farthest."

All the younger boys narrowed their eyes, scanning the water. None seemed to question if there was any truth to Bruno's statement. Each seemed to be looking for a frog with a lot of warts.

❖ ❖ ❖

"Should we go with the boys?" one of the frogs asked Kröte.

Kröte quickly replied, "Yes, let's go! It'll be fun."

Just then, Fritz grabbed Kröte.

A big smile appeared on Fritz's face, almost matching the grin on Kröte's.

CROAK!

-3-

Lache Lake Monsters

"The little girl ran through the woods as fast as she could. She tried to avoid tripping over the fallen branches and tree limbs. She hoped that the creature from the lake had not followed her. She kept looking back over her shoulder. A shadow was behind her.

"The girl was not sure if it was the green monster, or something else—*maybe something worse*, she feared. She kept thinking about how the creature's hand felt when it tried to grab her. It was cold, slimy, and felt dead. *It felt like a body without the skin,* she thought.

"*I am not going to escape*, the girl lamented. She wished she had taken off running when she first heard the eerie groan. *Why did I have to investigate? I should have just run.* The girl had thought that someone was hurt.

"When she had gotten closer, she realized that whatever it was—it was not fully human. Its body was shaped almost like a man, with arms and legs, but it was green and had scales like a fish. *Maybe it was human at one time*, she thought.

"The girl saw a cabin in the distance. *I'll run to the cabin and get help!* The girl was breathing heavily now. She could hear the monster drag dirt with its feet as it moved forward. Somehow, she got a burst of energy and ran even faster toward the cabin.

"She hoped that the door was not locked. She was now at the front of the cabin. The creature was still behind her but did not seem to like being exposed by the moonlight. The creature preferred the dark. The girl did not hesitate. She grabbed the doorknob."

"Oh, no!" All the younger kids that were gathered around the campfire at Lache Lake shrieked at the telling of the scary story.

The Camp Counselor telling the story smiled. His teeth glowed orangish-red from the light cast by the crackling fire.

The Camp Counselor seemed pleased with his storytelling.

It seemed that the more afraid the kids appeared, the spookier the Camp Counselor made the story. It was dark. Owls were hooting, and small animals were scurrying between the trees. The campers huddled as they listened to the campfire story.

Fritz and the younger boys had gotten back from swimming with the frogs a couple of hours earlier. Everyone thought that Fritz was quiet at dinner, unusually quiet. Some of the boys joked about Fritz having to fork over his dessert for losing at rock skipping.

Fritz sat still around the campfire with the other boys. Bruno shrieked louder than the girls, listening to the story.

Clara smiled as she listened. The story reminded her of the times she traveled deeper in the Black Forest.

She thought about King Dustin and Princess Sugar Plum. Mozart was now a year old, no longer a puppy. She had wanted to bring him to camp, but dogs were not allowed.

Clara was so glad that Queen Nordika, the Snow Queen of the Land of Snow, gave Mozart to her last summer. Queen Nordika had said, "It is a special gift, Clara. You have, once again, displayed great bravery."

Clara had thought that Mozart looked just like *The General*, the white shepherd canine that was the leader of Queen Nordika's royal guard. Later she found out that Mozart was one of The General's puppies.

Clara remembered being shocked when Mozart first spoke to her. She had forgotten that the magical butterflies had granted her wish. She had wished to be able to talk with animals, like King Dustin.

Although he was 'Prince' Dustin then, Clara recounted. After that, Clara was able to speak with animals, just like everyone else that lives Deep in the Black Forest.

Clara enjoyed speaking with animals. Many of the animals near her Uncle Drosselmeyer's old mill were from Deep in the Black Forest and would hold conversations with her.

Whenever Clara visited her Uncle Drosselmeyer, she would sing along with the songbirds and chatter with the cats.

Clara grimaced, recounting some of the creatures and specters she and her friends encountered last summer. She quickly thought about Drachenmeyer, her Uncle Drosselmeyer's wicked twin brother. She hoped that Drachenmeyer had not found a way to escape from Niedertrachtig Castle.

Clara thought back to Egon. Vicious and vile, Egon was King of the Land of Mice. She then thought about how her Uncle Drosselmeyer had turned Egon into a little white mouse. Clara chuckled, remembering. She was sure that lands Deep in the Black Forest were much better off without Egon.

"AAAAAAGH!" Several campers shrieked.

Clara snapped back from her thoughts. It was the end of the campfire story. The camp counselor looked pleased.

"Everyone. Go to your cabins. We have many activities planned for tomorrow," the camp counselor said as he thoroughly extinguished the fire. The firepit went black.

Once the fire was out, the twinkling stars glimmered even brighter, and the full moon shone like a glowing ball. Otherwise, all was pitch black at Lache Lake.

The younger girls clung to each other as they made their way through the dark forest. "That was scary, Clara," Ada said, panting out of breath. Ada was eight years old and was one of the two younger girls assigned to Clara's cabin.

"It was just a story, Ada. There are no green monsters," Clara said. However, Clara knew green creatures did exist *deeper* in the Black Forest. "You will be fine." Clara bent down and gave Ada a comforting hug.

Fritz and the younger boys walked closely behind the girls. Clara was surprised.

Fritz seemed anxious after hearing the campfire story. *Nothing usually scares Fritz*, Clara thought. *It must have been a really spooky story*. Clara walked slower so that Fritz and the other boys could keep up.

After a short walk, all the campers made it back to their cabins.

"Uhm, good night, Clara," Fritz said, rubbing the side of his face. He avoided looking at Clara.

That campfire story must have really spooked Fritz, Clara thought.

"Good night, Fritz," Clara said.

Fritz walked with Bruno toward their cabin. When he got to the door, Fritz looked back and smiled at Clara before entering. His eyes gleamed.

Clara smiled back at Fritz. *Fritz doesn't seem afraid anymore,* she thought.

Clara, Marie, Ada, and the other girls who shared Clara's cabin were chatting and laughing as they entered the log structure.

"Good night, Clara," Ada said, peeking up from her pillow.

"Gook night, Ada. Sweet dreams." Clara said with a smile.

Animals and insects sang a lullaby in the background as the girls fell soundly asleep. Owls hooted, crickets chirped, and katydids sang.

Except for the sound of the animal chorus, all was quiet at Camp Lache Lake.

❖ ❖ ❖

Ada jerked awake.

What was that? Something is in here! Ada panicked. She glanced over at Clara. Clara was sound asleep on the cot next to hers. Ada did not want to wake Clara, so she pulled the covers up over her body. She tried to hide from whatever was inside their cabin.

Ada trembled, thinking about the green monster in the campfire story. She tried to be as still as possible as she listened for movement in the room.

After a few moments, Ada lowered the covers enough to peek. She was breathing heavily, and her body was prickled all over with goosebumps.

Ada glanced at the other girls. Eight of them shared the cabin. All the other girls were still asleep. *Maybe it was nothing*, Ada thought. Ada then laid back down and pulled the covers up to her eyes. She soon drifted back off to sleep.

During the night, the moon shifted and glowed directly into the cabins' open windows. The wind also picked up. All the animals seemed to be asleep, along with the campers. It was the time of night when all the creatures, *living and dead*, roamed.

After some time, Ada jerked awake *again*. She shook underneath her covers, peeking out. It was dark inside the cabin. She could barely see. Ada heard the strange cries again!

BRAHNK   BRAHNK   BRAHNK

"What was that?" The other younger girl sharing the cabin gasped.

Deep, hoarse, throaty cries were coming from all around them. The moans got louder and louder!

"It sounds just like the monster from the story!" Ada shrieked.

❖ ❖ ❖

BRAHNK   BRAHNK   BRAHNK

All the girls in the cabin woke up hearing the sounds of the creature.

"Did you hear that?"

"What is it?"

"We're surrounded!"

"Stay in your beds," Clara said with grave concern, leaping from her cot. *Something is not right*. Clara walked around the room, inspecting. The frightful sounds continued.

BRAHNK   BRAHNK   BRAHNK

The girls panicked.

Clara tip-toed around the cabin, investigating. Clara was a lot braver than she had been a year earlier. She had experienced far worse Deeper in the Black Forest.

"Something's in here," Clara sighed. *Something is wrong, very wrong*, she thought.

"It's that monster from the lake!" Ada screamed.

"It's in our cabin!"

"It's gonna get us!"

"Be careful, Clara," Marie said. Her eyes darted around the room.

"I will," Clara replied, sounding calm but cautious. Whatever it was, Clara knew she had to protect the other girls.

Clara pulled out her crystal stone necklace from underneath her gown. King Dustin had given it to her the first time she ventured Deep into the Black Forest. It had magical powers.

"I have to protect the girls," Clara said silently.

BRAHNK   BRAHNK   BRAHNK

Clara stepped softly around the room. She thought about the wicked Wizard Drachenmeyer. She hoped that Merlin's magical stones, which kept the wicked wizard imprisoned, had not been removed.

I will not let Drachenmeyer hurt my friends, Clara thought, determined. Looking down at her crystal stone necklace, Clara noticed the stone glowed amber.

However, just then, something shot up in the cabin! It was quick. Clara could not fully see it.

Clara stood firmly on the floor, scanning the room. "Stay back!" Clara said to the other girls.

Then, another creature shot up—this time on the other side of the cabin.

"I just saw it!"

"They are after us!" Ada shrieked.

"They are too fast! We won't be able to escape!"

"The monsters are going to get us!"

"Clara, watch out!"

-4-

The Ice Palace

For the first time in a century, Sorceress Serihilda was flying above the other realm Deep in the Black Forest. The silver moon was exceptionally bright tonight. It was as though the moon was trying to impress the Sorceress. Serihilda nodded her approval.

The warm summer breeze from earlier in the day was overcome by the sharp stillness of the night. Serihilda's eyes glowed a brilliant purple. Her pupils looked like beams of light, piercing the sky as she flew across the atmosphere.

"Pathetic!" Serihilda said, glaring at the forest below. "I can't believe what Drosselmeyer has done. This realm of the Black Forest is not even recognizable."

A century ago, elements of the eerie and frightful Dark Forces were evident throughout all the lands of the Black Forest. From the sky above, Serihilda saw tall evergreen trees and winding rivers. Gushing waterfalls flowed from the mountains.

"Drosselmeyer ruined the Black Forest!" Serihilda said aloud. She did not see a specter nor ghoul. Not a spirit nor ghost was in sight. She didn't even see any of the wolves that walk on their hind legs. She attributed that to the fact that it was not yet a full moon. *Or, maybe they are not in this realm anymore either,* she thought.

"Simply pathetic!"

Serihilda saw giant mice, six-legged creatures with spiked tails, and other animals. However, she did not see any of the beasts or phantoms like the ones in her realm. *This is not the Black Forest,* she lamented.

Sadness shone in Serihilda's eyes. *Why would Wizard Drosselmeyer suppress the Dark Forces?*

Although Serihilda despised the trolls, she reasoned, *Even they are better than what I see here.*

A century ago, Wizard Drosselmeyer used very ancient magic against all the Dark Forces, including Sorceress Serihilda. The spell included the wizard's evil twin brother, Drachenmeyer.

The incantation took away their ability to journey to the other realm in the forest.

However, last year, Drachenmeyer found a way to undo the spell cast by his brother.

Within the year, Drosselmeyer's spell was completely undone. Serihilda and all the Dark Forces were released from the incantation.

Herr Drosselmeyer was unaware that Drachenmeyer had used Merlin's magical stones to undo the spell. And now it was too late.

"This place no longer even feels like the Black Forest," Serihilda shrugged as she traveled above the trees.

"A century of damage," Serihilda continued.

"I concur, Sorceress," Krieger said through his thoughts, reading Sorceress Serihilda's mind.

Although the giant Ogre was not traveling with Serihilda, they communicated through their thoughts by reading each other's minds.

"Hello, Krieger," Serihilda responded with her mind.

"Hello, Sorceress," Krieger replied through his thoughts.

"There's a palace with a moat in the distance," Serihilda said. "It's at the foothills of the mountain."

Krieger responded, "You must be in the Land of Snow. The structure you reference is the Ice Palace."

Serihilda cringed. "Land of Snow? There's no snow here. The so-called Ice Palace does not have not one crystal of ice. The palace is made completely of stone. Pathetic!"

"No snow. That would be correct," Krieger responded. "By my calculations, the last snowfall should have been forty-five days ago. The name of the land is somewhat ironic, I suppose. One would expect snow year-round."

"There's none, zero, zilch, keiner!" Serihilda emphasized. "That is the first thing I am chang—"

"Now, Sorceress," Krieger interrupted, "you said that you would just canvass the area on this trip."

"Just a little dusting of snow would hardly be noticed," Serihilda reasoned, raising her eyebrow and twitching her lip.

"I guess it will melt when the sun rises," Krieger conceded.

"Of course," Serihilda said, rolling her eyes. Sometimes she felt that the Ogre was too analytical.

Krieger continued, "We do not want anyone to be alerted that the Dark Forces have been released from Drosselmeyer's spell."

"Nobody will suspect a thing," Serihilda responded. "Just a little snow. What would be the harm?"

SNAP! Serihilda then snapped her fingers. Purple dust floated into the air.

Magically, soft billowy snowflakes began falling from the sky, dusting the land.

Serihilda frowned. The Sorceress still was not pleased.

SNAP! Serihilda snapped her fingers again.

"Are you still there, Sorceress?" Krieger said, sounding confused.

Serihilda had momentarily blocked her thoughts from Krieger. The Ogre was no longer able to read Serihilda's mind.

With a twinkle in her eye, Serihilda snapped her fingers, yet again. **SNAP!**

Just as before, purple dust floated into the air.

"That's much better!" Serihilda nodded approvingly as snow fell from the sky over the land.

❖ ❖ ❖

The General rushed to Queen Nordika's bed-chamber in the Ice Palace. The shepherd's tail extended like a sword. His teeth were exposed, and his fangs dripped drool. The General's eyes were cold and black.

Something was seriously wrong in the Land of Snow. The General of Queen Nordika's Royal Guard was not easily disturbed.

Queen Nordika, the Snow Queen, had already awakened. She was surveying the grounds from her bedroom window.

The Snow Queen stood motionless. Her porcelain-like face glowed under the moonlight like a bust of stone. The white silk gown she wore matched the color of her hair. Her gown and hair blew behind her as she looked through the glass pane. Only her eyes displayed concern.

The General said in a grave tone, "Something caused a sudden snowstorm, Your Highness." He continued, "It had to be some sort of enchantment. Nothing else could have done this."

The Snow Queen nodded. "Yes. I would have to agree. It never snows this time of year. And it happened so quickly. The mounds of snow seemed to just magically appear."

The General speculated with raised brows, "Drachenmeyer?"

"Maybe worse," the Queen replied.

"Worse?"

"None of the people, animals, or creatures from our realm could have done this. It has to be an enchantment," Queen Nordika said.

"Hmm. That would imply the Dark Forces," The General said.

"Yes," Queen Nordika acknowledged.

"That would mean—"

Queen Nordika nodded before The General could complete his sentence.

The General continued, "... that Herr Drosselmeyer's spell has been broken."

"That appears to be the case." Queen Nordika cast her eyes outside the window. "The Dark Forces must have entered our realm."

The General gritted his teeth.

"We must prepare," Queen Nordika said. "I will inform Herr Drosselmeyer. Our realm in the Black Forest is in peril."

Before the Queen walked away from the window, the wind whipped violently. The gust howled, screeched, and wailed. The storm sounded like wild animals under attack.

The torrent of flakes came down heavy and fast! Within moments, the Snow Queen was no longer able to see out of her bedroom window. It was covered in snow.

The snow continued its vicious attack on the castle. It thrashed the walls and engulfed the entire castle like a cyclone.

The stone palace swayed from the powerful force. The castle sounded like it would collapse.

WHOOOOOOOOOOOOOOOOOOOOSH!

"We must stop the Dark Forces," Queen Nordika exclaimed, charging out of her bed-chamber. The General followed. His eyes were so black, so intense that one could almost see his soul.

Suddenly—shattered glass from the windows flew across the room. A strong gust of wind followed. It blew snow directly into the bed-chamber. Just as quickly, the snow turned to ice.

Within a blink of an eye, Queen Nordika's bed-chamber was iced over. It looked like the inside of an igloo.

Queen Nordika looked back over her shoulder. She spotted a single white dove flying outside her bedroom window. It seemed unaffected by the storm.

The small bird blended in with the crystal white snow. If it were not for its piercing purple eyes, the dove would not have been visible at all.

"We don't have much time!" Queen Nordika said as she stared at the white bird with purple eyes.

The General stood up on his hind legs and howled at the dove.

Then a haunting wail was heard. It came from the woods. The violent storm awakened all the nearby animals and creatures, Deep in the Black Forest.

"This is just the beginning."

-5-

Creatures Everywhere

All the girls in the cabin, except Clara, screamed! "It's that creature from the campfire story!"

It was early in the morning. The sky was gray and gloomy. The sun was shining brightly somewhere else in the world.

"It's over here!"

"They are under our beds!"

"It touched my foot!"

"It tried to grab me!"

"They're everywhere!"

The creatures were now shooting up all around the dark cabin. The older girls ran around, trying to dodge them. Ada screamed, holding tight to her pillow. The other young girl cried underneath her blanket.

Clara chased after the creatures, trying to stop them from attacking. Nevertheless, as soon as one popped up, it vaulted across the room. She could not run fast enough.

Clara panted out of breath. She did not know how many creatures were in the cabin. However, Clara was determined to save the girls.

"They are fast. Stay back!" Clara shouted.

The girls did not stay back. They screamed as they ran from the creatures. The creatures grunted as they chased after the girls.

BRAHNK   BRAHNK   BRAHNK

"The girls aren't as fun to play with as the boys," Kröte croaked as he shot up off the floor in the girl's cabin.

"The girls don't want to play with us," another toad replied.

"Whenever I leap, they run away."

"I heard that boy say it would be fun, hiding us under girls' beds."

"Hey Kröte, the girls don't like playing tag."

"They're no fun."

"I had more fun with the boys."

Clara's jaw dropped as she listened to the toads' conversation. "Kröte?" Clara said, repeating the name she heard.

"CROAK!" Hearing the girl speak, the toads gulped with surprise.

"I think that girl heard us," Kröte whispered.

"Who is Kröte?" Clara said in a stern voice with her hands on her hips. She tapped her foot, waiting for a reply.

Kröte's bulging eyes blinked as he looked at Clara's foot. The frog tried to slip away under a bed.

Before Kröte could escape, Clara reached down and picked him up in the palm of her hands. All the other girls gasped.

"Are you Kröte?" Clara said. Clara's voice was soft but forceful.

"Yes, I'm Kröte," the toad uttered.

The sun was now beginning to rise. Light filtered into the cabin.

The girls in the cabin opened their mouths wide, watching Clara talk to the toad.

Clara held the toad close to her face.

"Croak! Croak! Croak!" the girls heard coming from the frog.

"Why did you chase the girls? You scared them." Clara scolded.

Kröte babbled, "We just wanted to play."

"Play?" Clara responded. "While we were sleeping?"

"The boys ... they hid us under the beds. They said it would be fun," Kröte replied.

"What ... boys? Who?" Clara demanded, narrowing her eyes.

"Uhm, I think the boy's name was Fritz. Yes, Fritz and his friends," Kröte responded.

"Fritz?" Clara asked.

"Yeah," Kröte replied.

"Hmm," Clara uttered, "I understand, now." All the other girls in the cabin glared at Clara with open mouths.

"Clara is talking to the green monster from the lake," Ada shrieked. The other young girl sharing the cabin hid further underneath her blanket.

Clara flushed, embarrassed. She then placed Kröte on the floorboards and gently pushed him toward the cabin's door. "Now go," she whispered, hoping nobody noticed her speaking to the toad again.

Kröte jumped as fast as he could toward the door and leaped out of the cabin. All the other toads followed.

BRAHNK   BRAHNK   BRAHNK

❖ ❖ ❖

Although the skies were dank and dark, the Spirits at Niedertrachtig Castle scattered. They went back to their daytime resting places.

Even though it was past the time to get up, Morning was not ready to start the day.

Wizard Drachenmeyer, the evil twin, glared into the sky from the top of the tower of the castle.

After a year of being imprisoned, he still had not found a way to escape the enchantment of Merlin's magical stones.

The wizard stared at something flying toward him.

"I don't suspect that would be my pitiful brother," Drachenmeyer snarled. A white mouse sitting on the ledge of the tower squeaked.

As the object flew closer to the castle, Drachenmeyer saw beams of purple light. The light illuminated the sky like beacons.

The closer the object got to the tower, the more human it appeared.

"That looks like—" Drachenmeyer smiled before finishing his sentence. The mouse squeaked louder than before.

Within moments the object in the sky was at the tower.

Wizard Drachenmeyer bowed deeply, holding the hem of his black cape.

"Sorceress Serihilda, it is truly my pleasure. However, I must apologize for my humble conditions."

Serihilda glared at the magical stones. Even she could not un-do their magic.

❖ ❖ ❖

Later in the morning, the Sun smiled down and peeked through the windows of the Dance Hall at Camp Lache Lake.

Clara, Marie, and the other dancers were warming up.

After a short time, Miss Patti stepped into the room. "Everyone, please be seated." She paused, allowing the girls and Rupert to take seats on the floor.

"If I call your name, you will be continuing to the Final Round for Girl Lead. All other dancers will be cast in the remaining roles. Some of you will need to be cast in boy roles. Rupert, as usual, you have been cast in the Boy Lead role."

A hush of silence fell across the hall as the dancers listened to Miss Patti.

"If your name is called, please line up here," Miss Patti instructed the girls with a wave of her hand.

Clara and Marie sat huddled with other dancers. All eyes were on Miss Patti and the papers in her hand.

The Ballet Mistress put on her spectacles. They hung on a chain around her neck. She then fumbled through papers. Her eyeglasses slid down her nose as she looked at her list of names.

Miss Patti then glanced at the dancers from the top of her lenses. She looked back down at her paper and slowly began calling names from the list.

"Sarah, please come to the front." A tall girl with red hair jumped off the floor. She walked, duck-feet style, with her toes pointed outward leading the rest of her body. Sarah stood with a happy smile next to Miss Patti when she reached the front of the room.

Miss Patti nodded at Sarah and then looked back at her list of names.

"Amelia," Miss Patti started. A girl with big brown eyes ran toward the front. Amelia was halfway across the room before Miss Patti finished speaking. "Please come to the front."

Miss Patti gave Amelia *the eye* before adjusting her spectacles.

The seated dancers anxiously waited for the next name to be called. Clara and Marie exchanged hopeful glances.

"Marie, please come forward."

Marie grinned with excitement. Clara hugged her friend as Marie rushed to the front. Miss Patti smiled approvingly at Marie.

The room was quiet again as everyone listened for the next name to be called. Miss Patti looked at her papers. She was about to read the next name when something caught her attention.

The Ballet Mistress stopped and glared. A disturbing look shone on her face as she looked out the window. All the dancers turned, following Miss Patti's eyes.

After a moment, Miss Patti shook her head, dismissing whatever it was that she thought she saw.

Although not even a minute passed, from the dancers' anxious expressions, it may have seemed like hours to them.

Sighs of relief echoed from across the room in anticipation of the next name.

"The last girl that will be moving forward to the Final Round for Girl Lead is Clara," Miss Patti said. "Clara, please come forward and join the other dancers in the front."

Clara's eyes went wide with surprise. She did not think that both she and Marie would move to the Final Round.

Clara stepped forward. She bit her lip to contain her excitement. Clara did not want to gush in front of the remaining girls that had not made it to the Final Round. Clara and Marie exchanged gleeful glances.

Next, a flurry of activities happened.

All the patience Miss Patti displayed earlier was lost. She signaled for the accompanist while rushing the selected dancers into the adjoining room for the Final Round of auditions.

❖ ❖ ❖

It was early in the evening. All the dancers were chatting and laughing as they exited the Dance Hall. The auditions had ended, and all roles were cast.

"I'm so sorry that you slipped, Clara," Marie said. "You danced beautifully before you fell."

"Thank you," Clara replied, hugging Marie. "I'm glad that you made Lead, though. You were amazing."

Marie blushed. "Thank you."

Clara then jerked her head as if she heard something in the woods. For a moment, she appeared alarmed.

Marie followed Clara's eyes. "Did you see something? You had that same look on your face before you tripped."

"Uhm, it was nothing," Clara responded, shrugging it off. However, she *had* seen something–or so she thought.

Clara had tripped while looking out the window during the Final Round. *That person outside the window of the Dance Hall looked just like King Dustin,* Clara thought.

Marie joked, "So, it wasn't any more creatures from the lake, was it?"

Both girls laughed as they thought about the frogs.

After both girls calmed down, Marie said in a curious tone, "You looked like you were talking with the frogs."

"Hmm, I was ... Uhm ... sort of," Clara responded.

Marie looked at Clara with bewilderment.

"Uh, like I do with Mozart, just basic commands–nobody can speak with animals. I was just being silly." Clara rubbed her nose and lowered her eyes.

Changing topics, Clara said quickly, "I'm hungry."

"Me too. I was too nervous to eat earlier," Marie replied.

"Mmm." Clara sniffed the air. "It smells like bratwurst and onions."

Marie nodded, "I hope they have pretzels." The girls stepped up their pace toward the Dining Hall. Other girls joined them, congratulating Marie.

Fritz and his friends ran past Clara and the girls. The boys looked like they were on a critical mission. They charged across the field toward the Dining Hall.

Clara wanted to speak to Fritz about his prank. Fritz was probably unaware that Clara knew that it was Fritz and his friends that planted the frogs in her cabin.

Clara just shook her head. She realized that it would be useless to speak with her brother about his prank. *He's probably already planning the next one,* Clara thought.

"Clara!"

Clara stopped and turned. She thought she heard her name called. She stared into the dense trees. "Did you hear that?"

Marie turned, "Hear what?"

Clara shook her head, "Uhm, it was probably nothing." The girls proceeded to the Dining Hall.

"Clara!"

- 6 -

King Dustin of Konfetenburg

"We're surrounded!" the Lieutenant yelled. King Dustin hesitated for a moment. He stared at the ghouls and thought about what his father would have done.

❖ ❖ ❖

King Dustin's parents, King Marc and Queen Arabelle went missing several years ago. Last year, by decree, on his fifteenth birthday, King Dustin was coronated King of Konfetenburg, the _Land of Sweets_.

Princess Leyna, the King's sister, two years younger than Dustin, is his only surviving family. King Marc and Queen

Arabelle adopted Leyna when she was a baby after her kingdom was attacked.

Twelve years ago, the princess's homeland, the Kingdom of Fliegen, the *Land of the Tree Fairies*, was ambushed. The Kingdom of Bosartig, the *Land of Mice,* ravaged the land.

King Marc's army arrived to thwart off the attack. However, it was too late. They only found a small baby girl, *a Tree Fairy*, crying in a bassinet.

When King Marc returned to his kingdom, he and Queen Arabelle adopted the baby girl and named her Princess Leyna. She was given the nickname *Sugar Plum* because of her reddish-brown curly hair.

When the King and Queen vanished, Princess Sugar Plum went back to her homeland to make a request of a magical Great Tree with extraordinary power. She asked the enchanted tree to grant King Dustin the ability to fly like Tree Fairies. The Great Tree granted Sugar Plum's request, and Dustin was then able to fly like his sister, Sugar Plum.

King Dustin and Princess Sugar Plum flew throughout their realm, searching for their parents. However, King Marc and Queen Arabelle were never found. Queen Nordika had said that their parents might have gone deeper into the Black Forest.

After several years passed, it was suspected that King Marc and Queen Arabelle did not survive.

❖ ❖ ❖

"We're surrounded!" the Lieutenant yelled, again—louder than before, possibly thinking that the King had not heard him the first time.

King Dustin jerked to attention, raising his sword high. Tall shadows with red glowing eyes lurked in the forest beyond the Kingdom of Konfetenburg. *They are getting closer.*

"We have one chance," King Dustin replied to the Lieutenant.

Sinister phantoms had been spotted in the middle of the night, waking the entire kingdom in the Land of Sweets. The creatures were not human.

The mysterious monsters had oblong-shaped heads and several arms attached to two spindly legs. Their arms flailed wildly in all directions like an octopus. The creatures were tall and slender, without a middle section to give them shape.

Red hot eyes blazed high on the phantoms' heads. Jagged teeth, stained yellow, protruded past their lips. Their mouths appeared to disappear into their faces.

King Dustin had assembled his army immediately once he was notified of a possible attack. "I will not let any harm come to Konfetenburg!"

The King was dressed in a blue and red uniform. The King's eyes shone like sapphire as he gazed into the river. A blanket of mist had settled over the water. *I must steer those creatures away from the kingdom!*

"We will lure them away from the Kingdom," King Dustin said, standing tall, angling the tip of his sword toward the mountains. The river flowed from Konfetenburg to the foothills of Mount Süßigkeiten.

The moon reflected off of King Dustin's light brown hair. His hair, curled slightly at his neck, drooped with perspiration. "We will take the path along the river, to the caves. The creatures will follow us to Mount Süßigkeiten away from the kingdom."

Extending his sword, King Dustin marched quickly. The blade from his sword cut into the darkness. King Dustin's army followed closely behind their King. The sound of their boots was precise. Not a foot skipped a beat.

As hoped, the ghouls followed King Dustin's army toward Mount Süßigkeiten.

"We will lose them in the caves," King Dustin said in a low voice, pulling at the hem of his jacket. Although his voice sounded confident, his eyes appeared concerned.

The creatures were not far behind. Their arms waved recklessly in the air. It looked as though their bodies did not have any bones—just cartilage and skin.

A low grunt seemed to be humming off the bodies of the creatures. It sounded like thousands of ghouls. Hearing the sinister sound, King Dustin and his army marched faster.

Within an hour, the army of Konfetenburg made it to the mountain. The Lieutenant waited for his orders. King Dustin's eyes were blank. He was not sure that his plan would work.

King Dustin ordered a small troop of men to remain outside the cave. All the other soldiers were directed to enter the cave. "They are close. Move quickly," he said.

"Yes, Sir." The large group of soldiers hastened their pace, entering the cave.

King Dustin gave the large group directions to a hidden chamber inside the cave. He told them that once inside the secret chamber, to follow the path. The path led to an opening on the other side of the forest, the King informed them.

"We must get ready," The King said, looking at the small group of soldiers that remained outside the cave. King Dustin instructed the troop to climb up the side of the cave and position themselves above its entrance.

The designated soldiers were ordered to wait for all the creatures to enter the cave. "Once the creatures are inside the cave, loosen the boulders," King Dustin said as he pointed at huge rocks nestled in crevices above the cave's entrance. "The avalanche of stones will seal the entrance, trapping the creatures."

The small group of soldiers climbed the walls of the cave. They had already retrieved limbs from nearby trees to loosen the rocks. The soldiers were now in place above the cave's entrance, ready and waiting.

After the last soldier from the larger group entered the cave, King Dustin faced his Lieutenant. "I need you to lead the soldiers through the cave and back to Konfetenburg."

The Lieutenant did not move. He looked at King Dustin with concerned eyes as if not wanting to leave the King's side.

Humm! Hearing the humming sound getting closer, both the King and the Lieutenant looked toward the woods.

King Dustin turned quickly back around. "I will fly to the top of the cave before the creatures get here. Go now!" King Dustin ordered.

"Yes, Sir," the Lieutenant said as he rushed into the cave.

King Dustin nodded. He then turned and flew above the entrance of the cave, joining the other soldiers. The small band of soldiers did not appear surprised that King Dustin chose to stay behind with them.

King Dustin peered into the trees. The ominous creatures were almost at the path that led to the cave. Seeing the ghouls on the path, King Dustin raised his sword above his head. In a low voice, he said, "When I lower my sword, release the boulders."

The creatures advanced. Their arms thrashed in all directions. Up close, their eyes looked like fireballs, King Dustin noticed. The low guttural moan rung in the King's ears.

King Dustin pulled at the hem of his jacket as he watched the ghouls proceed toward the cave.

Suddenly, King Dustin jerked his head. He saw something. The King narrowed his eyes for a sharper look.

King Dustin thought he saw a woman. A figure that looked like a lady stood in the middle of the ghouls. Worry immediately shone on King Dustin's face. *The creatures captured a lady!*

Sweat dripped down King Dustin's forehead. King Dustin thought back to when Egon, the King of Mice, kidnapped Sugar Plum.

"I have to rescue her from those creatures," King Dustin swore as he stared at the ghouls surrounding the lady.

The glow from the stars illuminated the creatures and their victim as they moved closer to the cave.

King Dustin glanced at the stars. Their glow seemed to flick on and off continuously. With each flick of the light, the creatures advanced–without their legs moving at all. Just their arms moved, flailing wildly in the flickering light.

The creatures surrounded the lady–she was helpless.

King Dustin glared at the phantoms circling the lady. *I have to get her away from them.* Deep down, the King knew it was a trap. *I have to save her.*

The King recounted when Sugar Plum was kidnapped. He remembered that it was a ploy to trap Clara. *The ghouls kidnapped that lady to get to me. They knew I would try to rescue her.*

As King of Konfetenburg, King Dustin understood why he was the target. *She should not have to suffer because of me,* he thought.

The lady looked up at King Dustin. Her face held the look of innocence as she gazed into King Dustin's eyes. She was wearing a beautifully embroidered satin gown that trailed behind. Her hair hung down her back.

King Dustin assumed the lady was just a few years older than himself. *Maybe twenty-years-old*, he assessed. *I have to come up with a plan quickly,* he thought, rubbing the side of his face.

The young lady stared at the King. She was probably hoping that the King would find a way to rescue her from the sinister creatures.

King Dustin stared back at the lady. He was distracted by her face. *There is something about her eyes.*

The lady's eyes glowed like beams of light in the darkness.

Suddenly, a chill ran down King Dustin's back. *Her eyes look evil,* he thought.

The young lady was now glaring at King Dustin. Her purple eyes never blinked. The soldiers huddled around King Dustin, appearing hypnotized. They seemed to be in a trance, or maybe an enchantment.

The lady cocked her head. "Today was just fun and games." She paused before continuing, "But I will be back."

The lady then pulled her long black and white hair over her shoulder. "I have more pressing matters to attend to now."

Standing in the middle of the ghouls, the lady curled her lips. "I hope you had a chance to say good-bye to Clara the last time you saw her."

"Clara?" King Dustin said, barely audible.

"Yes. Drachenmeyer told me all about Herr Drosselmeyer's *beloved* niece. I will be visiting Clara soon." The lady then snapped her fingers. Purple dust floated into the air.

POOF!

The ghouls then turned to dust and floated away.

King Dustin did not utter a word. He stared at the lady in disbelief.

"By the way, my name is Serihilda." The lady stood straight with a piercing strength King Dustin somehow missed before.

"Sorceress Serihilda," she stated with emphasis. "You should learn how to greet a lady properly instead of gawking."

The Sorceress then lifted herself off the ground. Her body went straight up in the air. Serihlida hovered in the sky for a few moments, glaring down at King Dustin.

Sorceress Serihilda then turned into a hawk and flew away. A cloud of purple dust trailed behind.

King Dustin looked into the horizon. Dread filled his eyes, and sweat fell from his forehead as he lifted his sword.

The King hoped that Sorceress Serihilda would return.

He hoped that she would not go after Clara.

He hoped that she would come back so that he could end this now.

After a while, King Dustin realized that all hope was lost. Sorceress Serihilda was not coming back.

-7-

The Tornado

Clara and Marie had returned to their cabin earlier in the day. Clara changed into a green pinafore dress, white short-sleeve blouse, and pantaloons. *I think I'll keep my dance shoes on*, Clara decided, pulling at the ribbons on her slippers.

"It's very dark out," Marie flinched, glaring out the cabin's window.

Clara glanced up. She had already noticed the dark skies and an eerie white cloud forming in the woods. *Hmm, something is terribly wrong*, Clara thought, joining Marie at the window.

Clara tried to hide her concern. "It looks like a storm is coming. It'll pass," Clara said.

"I've never seen a storm do that," Marie said. Fear shone on her face. Throughout the forest, the overcast skies turned everything an ominous gray. Strangely, a cloud of white was dead center.

"It's probably just going to rain." Clara stared at the menacing cloud in the middle of the darkness.

Marie nodded. "B-but what is that?" Marie said, pointing. The white funnel cloud moved through the trees like a ghost through a door.

That is not a storm. Something worse— Much worse, Clara concluded.

Trees knocked. Leaves violently blew in the air. Branches slammed against the ground. It sounded as though a thousand galloping horses were running through the woods. Marie covered her ears.

Then—pandemonium erupted amongst the campers! Screaming voices came from all directions.

Girls ran as fast as they could toward the Dance Hall.

Young boys jumped around, full of excitement. They appeared oblivious to the impending danger. Older boys stood in disbelief, pointing at the tornado.

A camp counselor shouted, "It's a storm! Everyone, get to the Dance Hall. Take cover NOW!" Counselors chased after the young boys, trying to corral them.

Before Clara and Marie had a chance to dash out of their cabin, two girls ran in. Panting, one girl said, "Miss Patti said to go to the Dance Hall! We'll be safe from the storm there."

Marie shrieked, "We better hurry!"

Clara replied, "I'm right behind you." However, she did not follow Marie. Clara did not go to the Dance Hall with the other campers.

Instead, Clara pulled her crystal stone necklace from underneath the top of her dress. *I have to stop it!* The amber color of the crystal stone was now dark blue. She knew the dark color meant impending peril.

Looking down at her enchanted necklace, Clara said, "Magic, please work!"

As though the funnel cloud heard, the cycling tornado whipped around and headed for Clara.

The crystal stone necklace levitated around Clara's neck. The color of the crystal was now jet-black.

-8-

Before the Full
Moon Rises

The violent tornado slashed through the trees at Lache Lake. It headed for Clara. A thunderous sound echoed throughout the forest.

Branches hurled through the air. Animals, large and small, stampeded in herds. Birds flew around in circles. The wind wailed and howled like a beast.

Unlike the animals, Clara ran as fast as she could toward the tornado. The crystal stone necklace was still hovering around her neck. Clara wished she had learned how to use its magical powers. *Magic, please work*, she said silently as she ran.

The forest was dark, eerily black. Only the white funnel was visible. Clara had to slow her pace to avoid running into trees.

The tornado stood still. Clara glared at the white funnel. *It's waiting for me.*

A horrible sound vibrated off the tornado. The noise bounced off the trees!

BWA-HA-HAH!   BWA-HA-HAH!

Clara stumbled, listening to the cackle. She didn't seem to notice that her necklace stopped hovering and had plopped to her chest.

"What is happening!" Her heart raced.

BWA-HA-HAH!   BWA-HA-HAH!

The tornado charged. It moved like a cyclone toward Clara.

Clara ran as fast as she could. She weaved through trees and jumped over rocks. *I have to stop it before it gets to the campgrounds!* Sweat splashed off Clara's face as she ran toward the tornado.

Clara had no idea what she would do once she reached the funnel. She hoped that the magic from her necklace would stop the tornado.

Blackness was all around Clara. She could only see a couple of yards ahead. She no longer heard the cries or howls of the animals. She was not sure if the animals got away or if the tornado got to them.

This must be the work of Drachenmeyer. Clara wondered if Drachenmeyer had escaped from Niedertrachtig Tower. She recounted her Uncle Herr Drosselmeyer saying, "No sorcerer can escape the magic of the stones."

Hmm, if this isn't the work of Drachenmeyer, then whom? Clara wondered.

The closer Clara got to the funnel, the larger it appeared. Clara kept running toward the tornado as she looked up. A few times, she tripped over fallen branches but was able to regain her balance.

Clara was now dangerously close to the funnel. Her hair and clothes were being blown, pulled toward the tornado. She looked down at the crystal stone of her necklace. *Magic, please work.* Clara pleaded with desperate eyes.

Clara watched, hoping that she would not be sucked into the tornado's grip. She watched as rocks and branches were yanked off the ground.

Clara clutched her necklace and closed her eyes. "Magic, please work."

Just then–

"Clara!" She opened her eyes, hearing someone, *or* some *thing*, shout out her name. She did not see the source of the caller.

"Clara! Clara! Clara!" Hearing her name again, Clara jerked around in all directions.

When Clara turned back around, the tornado was directly in front of her. The funnel had taken the shape of a face. Clara looked up at the face of the tornado. She clutched her necklace even tighter. *Magic, please work.*

Clara trembled, facing the tornado. "I am not going to let you hurt Fritz or the others!" she said in a shaky voice. She then pointed her necklace at the tornado. Clara shielded her eyes from the blinding black light cast from the crystal stone. "Magic, please work!"

The funnel stopped swirling.

For a moment, Clara felt relieved. She blew out the side of her mouth.

But, then—

The face of the tornado lunged at Clara.

"Magic, please work!" Clara pleaded, holding the necklace.

"CLARA!"

Clara jerked around. *That voice sounds like—*

Before Clara could complete her thought, she saw King Dustin fly toward her, calling her name. Princess Sugar Plum, Bronson, and Mozart were flying beside the King.

With the force of his energy field, King Dustin swooped Clara off the ground and into the air. Within moments Clara was out of the grasp of the tornado and in the sky.

Clara's heart raced as she peeked at the forest below. They were flying so fast that everything was blurred. Within moments they were far away from Lache Lake.

Clara could not speak. She was so happy to see her friends but could not say the words to let them know.

King Dustin looked over at Clara. "Are you all right, Clara? We got here as fast as we could."

Clara was breathing deeply. She nodded and smiled at King Dustin. She could not help but notice how much older the King looked. Although his hair was disheveled and his shirttail had come out of his pants, he looked like a brave warrior, Clara thought.

King Dustin said, pulling at the hem of his jacket, "The Dark Forces have been released. We only have until the full moon rises to defeat them. That is just two days from now!"

The End
of Act One

"We march these woods, one-hundred strong."

ACT 2

- 9 -

The Enchanted Black Forest

"*Twinkle, twinkle, little star.* How I wonder what you are! Up above the world so high ... " Clara hummed.

They were still flying above the Black Forest. Clara awakened to a galaxy of twinkling stars flickering like diamonds in the velvet sky. She had drifted off to sleep sometime after they left Lache Lake.

"Are you awake, Clara?" King Dustin said, glancing over.

Clara nodded.

"You were asleep for a while," Mozart barked.

Clara thought about the tornado. Worry shone on her face.

"We were afraid that we might be too late," King Dustin said solemnly. "We flew at lightning speed once Mozart told us where you were."

Clara smiled at everyone. "Thank you for rescuing me."

"I am glad we got to you in time!" Mozart responded, jumping up to lick Clara's face.

"Your Dad would be quite proud of you, Mozart," Clara said, referencing The General. Mozart wagged his fluffy tail.

Although Mozart looked and sounded as fierce as The General, his father, Mozart was more puppy than dog. Mozart barked as he continued to lick Clara's face.

Clara was glad that the magical butterflies granted her wish last year, allowing her to be able to speak with animals.

However, the animals that live in Clara's hometown do not know how to talk with people. They scamper away whenever Clara gets too close.

While flying, Clara and Princess Sugar Plum had time to catch up and chat about their lives over the past year. They are great friends and consider themselves sisters. Both girls matured considerably over the past twelve months. Although excited, their conversation no longer included giggly laughter.

Taking advantage of a break in the chitter-chatter, King Dustin interjected, "I need to tell you something, Clara." The King gripped tight to the handle of his sword, still in its sheath.

Clara looked at the serious expression on King Dustin's face. Last year, when the King had told Clara that Egon kidnapped Princess Sugar Plum, the King wore that same stark look, Clara recounted.

"The Black Forest and all of its inhabitants are in danger," King Dustin said.

Clara listened. Worry filled her eyes.

King Dustin proceeded to tell Clara about the release of the Dark Forces from Herr Drosselmeyer's spell that he had cast a century ago.

The King explained that Herr Drosselmeyer's evil twin brother, Wizard Drachenmeyer, used Merlin's magical stones to release the Dark Forces.

The King continued, "Queen Nordika had said that Drachenmeyer must have initiated the release of the spell before he became imprisoned at Niedertrachtig Castle."

Clara recalled her Uncle Drosselmeyer telling them about the spell he had cast that prevented the Dark Forces from entering the other realm in the forest.

The King elaborated, "The Dark Forces will wreak wickedness on all the kingdoms and lands. The lives of the people and animals that live in our realm of the Black Forest are in danger. We must stop the Dark Forces before the full moon rises."

Clara stuttered, "A-r-r-r-e, you saying that the Dark Forces have been released? That the evil creatures and spirits like the Ladies of Tanzer Lake are free to roam?"

"Yes. And also, an evil enchantress, Sorceress Serihilda."

Clara choked, recounting her horrible experience with the Spirits at Tanzer Lake.

The spirits masked their true selves behind the faces of *Lovely Ladies* while playing music and dancing. Clara's magical necklace protected her by zapping the lady spirits with a powerful blast when they charged. The spirits eventually gave up and flew away.

Clara glanced down at her necklace. The crystal stone glowed a brilliant amber hue. Clara sighed. She knew that the crystal stone would turn black to protect her from evil before they completed their mission.

Clara tried to smile despite the perils that lay ahead. She looked down at the majestic evergreens in the forest below. *We must save the Black Forest,* she vowed.

After a moment, Clara said, "That scary Tornado at camp, was it caused by the Dark Forces?"

"Yes," King Dustin replied.

"But why would the Dark Forces be at Lache Lake?" Clara asked, confused.

King Dustin did not immediately answer. The King shot a glance at Sugar Plum.

Princess Sugar Plum looked at Clara with concern.

Clara gulped. "Oh, because of me."

"Queen Nordika believes that Sorceress Serihilda went to Niedertrachtig Castle," King Dustin remarked.

"That's where Wizard Drachenmeyer is imprisoned, right?" Clara asked, raising an eyebrow.

"Yes," Bronson answered.

"Queen Nordika said that Drachenmeyer probably informed the Sorceress about how he was captured. The Queen said that Drachenmeyer most likely told the Sorceress about you, too," King Dustin said.

"Sorceress Serihilda is out for revenge against Herr Drosselmeyer because of the spell he cast over the Dark Forces," Princess Sugar Plum added.

"The Sorceress came to the Land of Sweets. She said—" King Dustin hung his head without finishing his sentence.

Clara's eyes went wide. "Did the Sorceress cause the tornado?" Clara asked.

"We are not sure," Sugar Plum responded.

"Probably, but there is no way to know for sure," King Dustin stated.

Clara replied, "That tornado was scary. I was trying to stop it from getting to Fritz and the other campers."

"Yes, it was quite fierce. It left as soon as we were in the sky. It was not after the other campers," King Dustin said.

Clara stopped in thought. She then asked in a concerned tone, "Do you think my hometown will be safe from the Dark Forces?"

"The Dark Forces are not interested in people that live outside the realms Deep in the Black Forest. They should be safe," King Dustin said.

Clara nodded.

King Dustin continued, "The Dark Forces might not have ventured to Lache Lake if you had not been there. They prefer to stay in the lands Deeper in the Black Forest."

Clara's eyes lowered. She felt terrible that she could have possibly brought harm to the other campers. She was glad that she did not go with Marie and the others to the Dance Hall. *The tornado would have followed me there. The other campers could have gotten hurt—or worse.*

"The lands **deeper** in the forest have no end. That realm just magically continues," Princess Sugar Plum added.

"The Sorceress and the Dark Forces dwell in the lands deeper in the forest **because** it is enchanted," King Dustin continued.

Clara nodded, "Oh, I understand. I think."

Princess Sugar Plum smiled. King Dustin nodded.

"But Egon, the Mouse King, isn't he from *your* realm in the forest?" Clara asked.

"Yes, he is from our realm. The Mouse King and his mice are not part of the Dark Forces. They are not enchanted or magical—just vicious and vile," King Dustin replied.

"And quite large for mice," Clara added.

"Yes. Most of the animals are larger in the Black Forest than they are in other places," King Dustin acknowledged.

Bronson added, "Our world is very different from your hometown, Clara."

Clara said, "Yes, indeed."

Mozart wagged his tail and barked, "*RUFF! RUFF!*"

Clara gave Mozart a big hug. Sometimes, Mozart barked, even though he had nothing to say. Mozart just likes to bark.

"*RUFF! RUFF!*"

As they flew across the lands, the sun began to rise. "Where are we?" Clara asked, looking down below. "It is so beautiful here!"

"We are in the Kingdom of Fliegen," King Dustin replied.

"This is where I am from, Clara!" Princess Sugar Plum exclaimed. "It is the *Land of the Tree Fairies*."

Clara exclaimed, "What a lovely place! Everything is so colorful and full of life. Even the grass looks to be a different shade of green. Much brighter. Cheerier. It looks like it glows."

"The Land of Fliegen is one of the most beautiful places in all of the Black Forest," King Dustin responded.

Princess Sugar Plum blushed with humble pride.

"We are going to land," King Dustin said as they began descending.

Hmmm. Clara noticed that everyone was now looking at her—*as if they shared a secret.*

-10-

The Enchantress

Events from earlier in the week...

It had just been a day since Sorceress Serihilda cast her spell over the Land of Snow. A carpet of green grass should have covered the rolling hills. Daffodil and bluebell flowers should have been popping out of the ground. Instead, snow was everywhere.

Although called the Land of Snow, the kingdom experiences all four seasons. *It did—* until now. It was now a Winter Wonderland in Spring.

Queen Nordika's army of white shepherd dogs frolicked and played in the glistening white powder. Their white fur blended in with the mounds of fresh snow.

Only their pink tongues were visible as the dogs romped and played.

Frolicking in the snow, the dogs did not look ferocious at all. They did not look like fierce soldiers. The white shepherds looked like oversized puppies dashing through the woods.

The dogs raced up the hills. They then turned their furry bodies into sleds as they came tumbling down.

The white shepherd dogs seemed truly delighted with the blizzard. "Ahhh!" they barked, sliding down the mounds.

❖ ❖ ❖

Wizard Herr Drosselmeyer was at the Ice Palace in the Land of Snow. He tried hundreds of incantations to undo the spell cast by Sorceress Serihilda.

Drosselmeyer chanted words only wizards knew. Nothing happened. He waved his magic wand. Again, nothing happened. He then mixed a strange concoction and drank it. The wizard belched bubbles. Still, nothing happened.

Although the Snow Queen preferred the snow, she had more severe concerns. The queen knew that this was just the beginning of the evilness the Dark Forces would bring.

Inside the parlor of the Ice Palace, Queen Nordika faced The General and stated, "The Dark Forces have to be stopped."

The General nodded with a solemn expression.

"Much is at stake," Queen Nordika continued. "All of the Black Forest could fall to their wickedness."

The General stiffened.

"We must prevent them from entering our realm," Queen Nordika said, determined.

"I am at your service, Your Highness." The General raised his right paw to his chest and bowed. "The Army of Shepherds will protect the lands Deep in the Black Forest."

"Do you think Mozart is ready?" Queen Nordika asked. "I need Mozart to accompany King Dustin and Clara. They need to go deeper into the forest, to the realm of the Dark Forces."

"In many ways, Mozart is still a pup," The General replied. "But he will do anything to protect Clara and the Black Forest."

The Snow Queen responded, "Good, his bravery will be needed."

The General nodded with pride.

Queen Nordika continued, "The Sorceress will not expect them, especially Clara."

The General agreed.

"Clara has excellent instincts. King Dustin will be able to use her assistance when they journey through the Black Forest," Queen Nordika stated.

The General stood, listening.

"With Princess Leyna and Bronson the Beaver, they will be a formidable group," Queen Nordika continued. The Snow Queen always called Sugar Plum by her formal name, Princess Leyna.

"That will be a good team to complete the mission," The General acknowledged.

"King Dustin has grown into a great leader. However, it will take every ounce of courage and wits for them to defeat the Sorceress," Queen Nordika said.

The General added, "Princess Sugar Plum can fly at incredible speed. That will come in handy. Although King Dustin can also fly, the Princess will be able to use her energy field to fly everyone. That will allow the group to travel much faster."

Queen Nordika agreed. "Yes. I am sure they will have moments when her speed will get them out of danger."

The General nodded.

"And Bronson will be able to use his sharp senses to guide them through the forest," the Snow Queen continued.

"Yes. Although Bronson has never gone Deeper in the Black Forest, he is the best beaver scout in our realm," The General said.

Queen Nordika paused, looking down. "Are we doing the right thing sending them alone?"

The General replied, "It is our only option, Your Highness. The Sorceress would not expect them. A surprise attack is the only chance we have to defeat her."

Queen Nordika nodded. "Today, I will go to the Kingdom of Konfetenburg to speak with King Dustin. He and the others will need to depart immediately."

"I will be happy to accompany you, Your Highness."

Just when the Snow Queen and The General were about to leave the room, Wizard Herr Drosselmeyer charged in, out of breath. "Sorceress Serihilda is a very powerful enchantress," the wizard said. "I tried everything, but I cannot change the weather back to Spring. I am unable to break Serihilda's spell."

Queen Nordika looked at The General with grave concern. Worry shone on her face.

If Sorceress Serihilda is more powerful than Wizard Herr Drosselmeyer, then King Dustin and Clara—. The Snow Queen did not complete her thoughts.

The General spoke as though he knew what the Snow Queen was thinking, "We have no other choice, Your Highness."

Queen Nordika agreed. "We must leave immediately for Konfetenburg."

Herr Drosselmeyer wiped his brow and said, "I will accompany you. There are some more details that King Dustin will need to know."

-11-

Land of the Tree Fairies

In the soft glow of the rising sun, bumblebees buzzed, and songbirds sang. A warm breeze blew gently in the Land of the Tree Fairies.

As Clara and her friends descended, the scent of wildflowers greeted them as if saying, "Welcome to the Kingdom of Fliegen."

Clara saw scores of Tree Fairies. The fairies flew gracefully between the large evergreen trees. Clara glanced at Princess Sugar Plum. "Your homeland is beautiful."

Sugar Plum smiled with the widest of grins. "Thank you, Clara."

The Tree Fairies shared Sugar Plum's brown skin tone. The color of their skin blended in with the trunks of the trees. Their hair was all different shades of brown. Some had reddish-brown hair, just like Sugar Plum. Others had dark brown. However, they all had curly locks that looked like sweet baby's breath flowers.

Clara thought the Tree Fairies flew like graceful swans. Some of the younger ones seemed to be playing tag. However, instead of running after each other, they leaped and pirouetted from tree to tree.

"We are landing over there, by that tree." Princess Sugar Plum pointed in the direction of a huge tree. "It is called the Great Tree."

The Great Tree was massive, even by Black Forest standards. It was the only tree in the land that was not of the evergreen type.

Some of its limbs had branches and vines that seemed to wind their way through the sky. The branches extended somewhere beyond the clouds—like a giant stalk.

The lowest vines hung and blew like a willow in the breeze.

Clara wondered if the Great Tree had a top at all. *Maybe it just continues—beyond the skies above.*

As they flew closer toward the ground, Clara braced herself. She wobbled when they landed. "Whew!"

Bronson grunted.

Mozart took advantage of the quick stop and rolled over a couple of times. "Whee!" Grass and dirt collected in his fur. He shook his coat. Dirt and dried leaves flew everywhere.

"Sorry," Princess Sugar Plum said, apologizing for the rough landing.

King Dustin said, "Princess Sugar Plum thought it would be helpful if you were able to maneuver through the lands in the forest."

Clara twisted her lip, obviously not understanding.

"Like me, Clara." King Dustin continued.

Clara smiled, but her eyes went from side to side. She did not want King Dustin to know that she still didn't understand.

Princess Sugar Plum chuckled, watching Clara's expression. "I am going to ask the Great Tree to grant you the ability to fly, Clara!"

Clara's mouth went wide. She finally understood. She shrieked, "Huh, I will be able to fly like you and King Dustin!"

"Yes," Princess Sugar Plum said.

Clara jumped up and down, hugging Princess Sugar Plum. The girls hugged and jumped for a long while, full of excitement. They sounded like their former twelve-year-old selves, full of giddy laughter and joy.

After the girls calmed down, Sugar Plum said, "Are you ready?"

Clara could not utter a word. She nodded her head several times, visibly shaking with excitement. *I will be able to fly like an eagle!*

When they reached the Great Tree, Princess Sugar Plum looked up. "Hello, Great Tree, remember me?" The branches of the tree stopped swaying as though at attention. The tree was motionless. Not a leaf moved.

Clara held her stomach. Her belly churned. Then a worried look shone on Clara's face. *I wonder if this is going to hurt?* Clara was not sure what to expect.

"Dear Great Tree of the Land of Fliegen, I have come before you today to request that Clara be granted the ability to fly … as you did for King Dustin," Princess Sugar Plum said, facing the tree.

The Great Tree did not respond. It remained motionless.

Princess Sugar Plum paused, then continued, "The Dark Forces, Deeper in the Black Forest have been released."

SUDDENLY, the limbs of the tree swayed violently and erratically. Clara was almost knocked off balance. Her hair blew wildly, covering her face.

Mozart barked and pricked his ears. Bronson's fur stood straight up around his neck. Only King Dustin and Princess Sugar Plum appeared calm.

After a moment, Princess Sugar Plum continued, "Clara needs to be able to fly to help defeat Sorceress Serihilda and the Dark Forces."

Everyone jerked their heads when they heard thunder. Soon, they realized that it was not thunder at all.

Clara trembled. Mozart pricked his ears. Bronson grunted. Princess Sugar Plum faced the Great Tree with hopeful eyes. King Dustin stood resolute.

"I WILL GRANT YOUR REQUEST!" The Great Tree spoke with an echo.

Suddenly, branches of the Great Tree extended. Its limbs moved like a snake and reached for Clara. The tree twisted its vines around Clara's body and lifted her off the ground.

King Dustin watched with concern. Bronson grunted. Mozart barked. Even Sugar Plum appeared worried.

Clara closed her eyes tight. *What is happening?* She trembled. A tingling sensation shot through her body.

The Great Tree then lifted Clara higher and higher off the ground.

Clara began to feel light-headed and dizzy. She thought she was going to pass out. *Did something go wrong?* Clara panicked.

A strong current of energy raced through Clara's body. Clara's heart pounded in her chest. Sheets of sweat poured down from Clara's body like a rainstorm. Clara's ears throbbed and popped. Clara thought her earlobes were going to explode.

Clara felt her body swirl.

SWOOOOOOOSH!

Clara wanted to open her eyes, but the force kept them closed. A bright light seeped underneath her eyelids. The light was intense. Clara closed her eyes even tighter! She feared that if she opened her eyes, she would be blinded.

SUDDENLY–Clara's body started convulsing, shaking viciously. When Clara could take no more–EVERYTHING WENT BLACK!

-12-

GONE! She Vanished!

Sorceress Serihilda watched as the Great Tree lifted Clara off the ground. Serihilda's purple eyes sparkled. The Sorceress stood behind a large evergreen, hidden from view.

The gusts of wind caused by the Great Tree blew Serihilda's long black and white hair. With her hair blowing wildly, Serihilda could have looked like a ghost floating amongst the trees.

"Not now," the Sorceress said, shaking her head. She then snapped her fingers.

SNAP! Purple dust floated into the air, and Serihilda's hair instantly fell straight down. The Sorceress did not want her hair to catch anyone's attention.

"Sorceress," Krieger interrupted, communicating to Serihilda through his thoughts. The Ogre was still at Zauberin Castle.

"Krieger, are you there?" Serihilda communicated back to the Ogre with her mind.

"Yes, Sorceress," Krieger replied. "Good move. Someone could have spotted your hair."

"And that would have spoiled all the fun," Serihilda quipped with gleaming eyes.

Krieger replied, "Sorceress, we do not want to make a mess of things. We can control things better here at Zauberin Castle."

"Yes, but–" the Sorceress said with a smirk.

SNAP! Serihilda snapped her fingers. Again, purple dust floated into the air.

"Serihilda, are you there?" Krieger said, confused. The Ogre could no longer read the Sorceress's mind.

"But, what fun would that be?" Serihilda laughed.

SNAP! After purple dust floated in the air, a thick white cloud started to form.

The cloud got bigger and bigger until it hid Serihilda. Within moments, the Sorceress was out of sight, hidden by the white cloud.

Then the cloud disappeared. Serihilda was not there either. GONE! She Vanished! The Sorceress disappeared.

On the ground, where Serihilda had stood, there was now a fluffy black and white rabbit. It had purple eyes. The rabbit scuttled toward the Great Tree—toward Clara.

❖ ❖ ❖

The limbs of the Great Tree slowly released Clara, unwrapping its branches from her suspended body. Clara slowly gained consciousness.

Peeking with one eye open, Clara gulped. She was floating in the air. Clara trembled, fearing that she was going to fall to the ground at any moment.

Breathing heavily, Clara opened up both eyes and looked below.

King Dustin and Princess Sugar Plum were watching with anticipation. Bronson had one eye covered with his paw. Mozart held his arms open and ready. *Good, Mozart. Just in case I fall,* Clara thought, relieved.

Clara felt the final branch releasing her body. *I am going to either fall or fly.* Clara crossed her fingers like she did when she was a little girl.

The last branch of the Great Tree released Clara from its grasp. Clara caught her breath, waiting to drop to the ground.

However, Clara did not fall. She floated in the air. "I'm flying!" Clara said.

Bronson yelled, "Yes, Clara! You are flying."

Mozart barked, jumping up and down, "You can fly!"

Glowing with glee, Princess Sugar Plum shrieked, "Just like King Dustin!"

"Fly down, Clara," King Dustin said, excited. His sapphire-blue eyes gleamed.

Clara floated in the air like she was in a lake of water. Even though she had not fallen, she was still nervous about being able to fly. She did not move.

"You won't fall," Princess Sugar Plum said convincingly.

Clara then took a deep breath. "Here goes."

Slowly, Clara moved her arms and legs. She willed herself to fly, and down she flew. Clara's eyes went wide as her body floated toward the ground.

"I can fly!" Clara shrieked. "I can fly just like King Dustin."

When Clara reached the ground, she fell to her knees. "I have to practice landing," she chuckled as she stood.

"You can fly, Clara!" Mozart licked Clara all over her face.

Clara gave Mozart a big hug and sat on the ground next to him. She looked up at Princess Sugar Plum for confirmation. "That was me flying, right?"

"Yes." Sugar Plum patted Clara's hair, smoothing it down. Clara's hair was wiry and stuck out in all directions, filled with static current.

"Just like me," King Dustin responded.

JUST THEN–a fluffy black and white rabbit hopped over to Clara.

"Look!" Clara said. "It's so cute." Clara picked up the rabbit, lifting it to her face. The rabbit's ears drooped, and it twitched its little nose.

"It has purple eyes," Clara said, hugging the rabbit.

"It's adorable," Sugar Plum said. The Fairy Princess then joined Clara on the ground and rubbed the rabbit behind its ears.

King Dustin said with curiosity, "Where did it come from? It was not here before."

Bronson grunted. Mozart barked. The beaver and shepherd seemed to sense something worrisome about the rabbit.

Clara looked up at Bronson and Mozart. "It's just a little bunny rabbit. It's harmless."

King Dustin smiled, looking down at the rabbit. The rabbit looked up at King Dustin and blinked its purple eyes. The King's smile froze in place.

"Hmm," King Dustin said, rubbing the side of his face. He looked down at the rabbit again. The King shook his head as if dismissing his thoughts. He knelt and petted the rabbit. "He is a cute little fella."

"Shouldn't we be going," Bronson said abruptly. The beaver glared at the rabbit.

Mozart barked in agreement, gritting his teeth. The dog's eyes did not leave the rabbit as Clara held the bunny in her lap.

Clara glanced at Mozart. She did not understand why the shepherd dog was acting oddly toward the rabbit.

"Yes," King Dustin agreed, looking into the horizon. "We have a long journey ahead of us. We will stop in the village to eat. Then, we must be on our way."

Princess Sugar Plum nodded.

Clara gently put the rabbit down. She rubbed the rabbit behind its ears one last time. Clara then patted the rabbit's tail, scooting it away. "Have fun, little rabbit," Clara said, smiling.

The rabbit looked up at Clara. "The fun is just beginning," the rabbit communicated in a sinister voice.

Clara jerked backward. The bunny had not moved its mouth. It was as though the rabbit was speaking to Clara through thoughts.

Clara looked up at her friends. None seemed to have noticed, not even Mozart. *Hmm, just my imagination,* Clara resolved.

The black and white rabbit with purple eyes then hopped away.

❖ ❖ ❖

After eating, Clara and her friends departed the *Land of the Tree Fairies.* It was the middle of the day, and they were back in the air.

Although Clara and King Dustin could fly, Sugar Plum used her energy field to fly everyone across the sky since the Fairy Princess could fly much faster. They were headed for the realm of the Dark Forces, Deeper in the forest.

Clara glanced down at the puffy clouds.

Princess Sugar Plum had said that if they flew above the clouds, that they would fly faster. Clara's heart raced as they zipped across the sky.

The clouds were so thick that Clara could not see anything beneath them. All she saw was white. Above them, below them, everywhere she turned, she saw white.

"The clouds look like snow-covered mountains," Clara said.

King Dustin agreed, "Yes, they do."

Mozart added, "Wouldn't it be fun if we could slide down the clouds!"

"That would be fun, Mozart. My dad takes us sledding every year after the first snowfall," Clara stated.

"We should be flying above lands Deeper in the Black Forest now," Princess Sugar Plum said.

"Yes, we are in the realm of the Dark Forces," King Dustin confirmed.

Clara shivered. She had almost forgotten about their mission.

King Dustin gripped his sword. "Once we enter the realm of the Dark Forces, we will need to move swiftly."

Bronson nodded, "Yes, the creatures will sense our presence."

"... and not just the animals." The King glanced at Clara and Sugar Plum. He gripped the handle of his sword tighter. King Dustin was very protective of Clara and Sugar Plum.

"We only have until the full moon rises tomorrow night to complete our mission." King Dustin reiterated.

Bronson grunted, exposing his front teeth.

Mozart growled, "I'm not afraid of no Sorceress."

Mozart is brave like The General. Clara smiled with pride.

Clara knew that she had to be brave, too. *I am brave,* she chanted, trying to convince herself. *I am brave. I am brave. I am brave.*

King Dustin had said that their success was dependent on surprising the Sorceress. Otherwise, *All will be doomed,* Clara thought.

"We can start descending," Princess Sugar Plum said. "We should be able to see the forest once we fly below the clouds."

WHOOSH!

Princess Sugar Plum used her energy field, pulling everyone with her to quickly descend from the sky.

Clara held onto the air as if it had handrails. Bronson grunted, and Mozart yelped. Everybody jerked, caught off-guard by the sudden motion.

"I did say we needed to move quickly," King Dustin chuckled. Within seconds, they had descended to the clouds.

"Something's wrong!" Clara shrieked. Clara tumbled against the clouds. It was a solid mass of ice. Clara gripped the sides of her dress and held on like it was a sled. Clara went down fast.

Clara could not brace herself. She kept sliding. Something had turned the clouds into snow and ice. Clara tried to fly, but she was powerless against the enchanted clouds.

"Oh, NOOOOOOOOOOOOOOOOOOOO!"

Clara shrieked as she slid down the slippery slope. She regretted saying that sliding down the clouds would be fun.

-13-

Falling

"What is happening!" Clara shrieked as her body continued to slide down the cloud. She felt like she was riding a toboggan. Her body twisted and turned, curved and dipped. Clara moved so fast. She could barely catch her breath.

"Hold on, Clara!" Mozart yelled. The shepherd dog sounded distant.

"The clouds turned into a solid mass," King Dustin said in a muffled voice. "Try to fly, Clara."

Clara tried to fly. She lifted her right foot, but it snapped back down. Clara could not release her body from the cloud. She kept sliding. A strange force was in control.

"Oh, no!" Clara screamed. The edge of the cloud was just a few feet away. Clara tried to fly. *We are falling from the sky!*

Clara tried to lift her left foot. She tried to fly. Within moments, Clara was hurling through the air. *Am I flying?*

THUMP!

Clara fell to a lower cloud. She was not flying. Clara's eyes stung as her hair slashed her face.

Clara's body whipped up and down the mounds. She tried to suppress the urge to throw up. "Ugh!" Warm ooze dripped down Clara's face.

Lifting her head, Clara saw the forest below. She hoped that they would land on the branches of the trees.

Then, she heard something. A frightful voice echoed through the atmosphere.

"Little girl," the angry voice called out to Clara.

"Huh?" Clara choked.

"Little girl," the voice repeated, louder than before.

"Mozart?" Clara hoped it was Mozart speaking to her. Deep down, Clara knew it was not Mozart.

"NO!" the voice thundered. "I AM NOT MOZART!"

Clara jerked, and her eyes went wide. She looked left, then right.

"DON'T YOU REMEMBER ME, LITTLE GIRL?" the voice continued.

Clara could not speak. She felt like her body was moving in slow motion.

"Clara!"

Clara thought that this time the voice sounded like King Dustin. The King did not sound close. *Maybe he landed on another cloud.* Clara shook her head before drifting into momentary shock.

"LITTLE GIRL!" the voice said, agitated. "DO YOU REMEMBER ME?"

Clara jolted back to the present. "I do not remember you. Are you the Sorceress?"

"DO I LOOK LIKE A SORCERESS?"

Clara looked around. She did not see anyone. She gulped, "Uh, no," Clara responded.

"LAST TIME, YOU TRESPASSED ON MY WATERFALL WITHOUT MY PERMISSION!"

Clara gasped. She recounted when she first journeyed deep in the Black Forest. She and King Dustin rode a boat down the river to get to the Land of Snow.

Clara recalled falling out of the boat as it went down a waterfall. She thought then that she heard a voice speaking to her. The voice was upset, she remembered.

"I'm sorry," Clara responded.

"YOU SAID THAT LAST TIME," the voice responded.

"My Friends," Clara started. She was worried about her friends as she recalled what happened to her last time. "Please do not hurt them. They are—"

Before Clara could finish her sentence, she heard the sound of eerie laughter echo off the cloud.

"AGAIN, YOU FAILED TO ASK MY PERMISSION."

Clara lowered her eyes and tried to lift her body. She replied, "I am sorry we fell on your clouds. Can we have permission to fly through the clouds?"

"NO!"

"Uhm, uh—" Clara desperately tried to find words.

Then a strong force pushed Clara's body off the cloud. Down she went. Clara fell from the sky!

HAHAHAHAHAHAHA!

The thunderous voice laughed.

Clara's eardrums popped as she somersaulted through the sky. Down and down and down she went. Clara spiraled from the sky.

Clara avoided looking down, so she looked left. Princess Sugar Plum was falling, too. "Oh, no!" Clara had hoped the others would have been spared.

Clara looked for King Dustin, Bronson, and Mozart. They were also hurling down from the sky.

It's all my fault. Clara felt responsible for not finding the words to be granted permission. "It's all my fault," Clara moaned.

HAHAHAHAHAHAHA!

The thunderous voice laughed again as Clara and her friends fell from the sky like spinning tops.

❖ ❖ ❖

At Zauberin Castle, Sorceress Serihilda and Krieger walked through a musty corridor in the dungeon. The Sorceress waved her hand, trying to air out the foul smell. Serihilda had returned earlier from the other realm in the forest.

"I have a surprise for you," the Sorceress said, speaking into a locked chamber.

Something was huddled in the corner of the dungeon. Serihilda's purple eyes glowed exceptionally bright in the darkness.

In the corner of the dungeon, two dreadful creatures stooped over. They raised their heads, hearing the Sorceress.

The figures were barely visible against the stone walls. They wore faded cloaks and hoods, hiding their faces and bodies. They smelled like they were dead.

Serihilda held her nose. "I need some fresh air." She then turned and walked away without telling the creatures what the surprise was. Krieger followed the Sorceress. He did not hold his nose. The smell did not seem to bother him.

The two creatures then huddled back into the corner of their chamber.

❖ ❖ ❖

Clara gasped for air as she fell from the sky.

The thunderous laughter stopped. The laughter's source either moved on or was no longer interested in Clara and her friends.

It probably moved on to deal with other trespassers, Clara thought.

Clara tried to lift her ankle. "Yes!" Clara said, raising her foot. Clara looked around and saw Princess Sugar Plum flying in the sky.

"Fly, Clara!" Sugar Plum said. "We can fly now."

Clara saw King Dustin flying. The King used his energy field to keep Bronson and Mozart in his air space. The animals floated alongside King Dustin.

Clara was no longer falling. She was flying! For fun, she extended her arms like an eagle's wings.

S*WOOSH!*

Clara and her friends flew down to the forest below.

Within moments, they arrived at their destination—the Realm of the Dark Forces, Deeper in the Black Forest.

Clara looked around and gulped.

March of the Trolls

We march these woods,
One-hundred strong.
Bellies empty,
But not for long.

To all the beings,
That cross our way,
You will surely,
Die today!

Singing and chanting were heard coming out of the forest. The voices were loud and deep. The tall grass hid the owners of the voices.

King Dustin lifted his finger to his lips. "We must be quiet," he whispered. After landing in the realm of the Dark Forces, Clara, and her friends barely had enough time to hide.

"Listen closely to the words in their song," Bronson said. "This must be the Land of Trolls."

"Trolls?" Clara whispered.

"Yes. Trolls are vicious creatures. Some say they are half-man and half-beast," Bronson replied.

Mozart barked.

SUDDENLY, the trolls stopped singing. All that was heard was the sound of animals sniffing their noses as though they were picking up a scent.

King Dustin lifted his finger to his lips again and pulled his sword out of its sheath. He then locked eyes with Bronson. Bronson acknowledged with a firm nod, raising his tail.

One of the trolls marched forward. The tall grass no longer hid the creature.

Clara was surprised that the troll was no taller than her brother Fritz.

Clara stepped back when she looked closer. The troll was mean and scary-looking. *It does look like an animal—or human,* she gasped.

The troll sniffed the air with its big nose. It lifted its right foot and pounded it into the ground. The earth shook.

THUD!

Birds on the nearby trees took off, shrieking as they flew. The trolls sang louder as they followed their leader out of the grass.

"It's an army," Clara said.

We stamp our claim,
With our big feet.
Then pick their bones,
And eat the meat.

We prowl our grounds,
So, all beware.
You cross our path,
We challenge your dare.

Clara cocked her head to listen. Suddenly, her eyes and mouth went wide.

Clara and Princess Sugar Plum looked at each other at the same time.

"I'll fly us out of here quickly," Sugar Plum said. Sugar Plum lifted her heels and hovered in the air. She sighed, frustrated when her feet fell back to the ground.

"My strength seems to be drained. I don't have the energy to fly." Sugar Plum lowered her head. "This is the first time this has ever happened to me. I'll have to regain my strength before I can fly again."

Clara knew that if Princess Sugar Plum could not fly, then neither she nor King Dustin could fly either. They all needed to build up their strength before they would be able to fly again.

Sugar Plum continued to try to lift her heels off the ground but could not. "Hopefully, my strength will be restored soon," she said, concerned.

Clara hugged Princess Sugar Plum. "It will." Sugar Plum smiled at Clara with downcast eyes.

The sound of pounding feet alerted them.

"We must leave, now," King Dustin said. The King narrowed his eyes, surveying the area.

Bronson pointed. "There's a path." A narrow path between the trees was on the right.

King Dustin shrugged. "They will expect us to go down that path." The King then looked at the dense trees.

"Mozart, find a way through the trees," King Dustin said. "Clara and Sugar Plum, go with Mozart. The trolls will not suspect that you have veered away from the path."

Mozart pricked his ears. "Yes, King Dustin." Mozart barked, "You can count on me."

King Dustin said, "I know I can, Mozart." The King looked down, "Bronson and I will be right behind you. I just want to cover our path, so they cannot tell the direction we are headed."

Clara and Princess Sugar Plum nodded.

Mozart raised his head high, sniffing. "This way, Clara and Princess Sugar Plum."

The girls followed quickly behind Mozart. Within moments they were out of sight, hidden by the dense trees.

King Dustin and Bronson used branches, sweeping the ground to hide their footprints.

"Ready? We will lure the trolls down the open pathway. Then the others will be safe. Had I told them the full plan, they would have never left our side," King Dustin said.

The beaver bowed. "I will be by your side, Your Highness."

"Let us go." King Dustin then darted down the open path. Bronson followed behind.

After a few moments, the path shook underneath King Dustin's feet. The King glanced over his shoulder. "Good. They are following us."

King Dustin did not seem to notice that a small band of trolls was splitting off from the larger group.

The smaller group marched into the dense trees—headed in the same direction as Mozart, Clara, and Princess Sugar Plum.

❖ ❖ ❖

Although the trees were dense, Mozart was agile. He weaved through the trunks of the evergreens like a smaller animal might. He looked back at Clara and Princess Sugar

Plum. They were not able to move as quickly as the shepherd dog.

"I'll slow down," Mozart said. The dog stopped to wait for Clara and Princess Sugar Plum to catch up. Although the dog's white fur had become tangled with dead grass and fallen leaves, his eyes retained their spark.

"We will be right behind you, Mozart." Clara panted, hastening her pace. She glanced back at Princess Sugar Plum. Sugar Plum was directly behind Clara. The trees were so dense that Clara could not see past the Princess. She wondered how far back King Dustin and Bronson were behind them.

Clara then turned back around. She ran even faster to catch up to Mozart.

Princess Sugar Plum looked over her shoulder into the trees. "I'm sure King Dustin and Bronson are not far behind," she said in a worried tone.

Mozart nodded. Clara and Princess Sugar Plum had caught up to the shepherd. Mozart then darted through the trees but at a slightly slower pace.

After Mozart and the girls had run for a while, they heard singing. It sounded distant from the direction of the open pathway. "It's the trolls," Clara panted, glancing back at Princess Sugar Plum.

Princess Sugar Plum responded, "They did go down the open pathway like King Dustin said they would do."

Clara nodded.

Princess Sugar Plum looked over her shoulder. "King Dustin and Bronson should be right behind–" Princess Sugar Plum's voice trailed off.

Hearing the pause in Sugar Plum's voice, Clara turned her head around. "Do you see King Dustin and Bron–" Clara gasped as she glared at something in the trees behind them.

❖ ❖ ❖

King Dustin and Bronson ran fast down the open path. "The trolls are close!"

A cloud of dirt and muck headed toward the King and Bronson. The dust was higher than the height of the trolls. The trolls' voices were loud as they chanted.

> *We'll watch you breathe*
> *Your very last breath.*
> *Gouge your eyes,*
> *And stomp you to death!*

> *We are the Trolls,*
> *Mighty and strong,*
> *We're coming for you,*
> *You won't live long.*

Hearing the close voices of the Trolls, King Dustin said, "They are faster than I thought."

Bronson grunted as he ran behind King Dustin.

The open path followed the terrain. It curved around the trees and dipped in spots.

Sweat splashed off King Dustin's face as he ran over rocks and maneuvered around fallen tree limbs.

Bronson kept his tail high to avoid tripping. He used his webbed feet to slide over the damp leaves that had fallen off the trees. The beaver, skating on the wet leaves with his webbed feet, was almost as quick as King Dustin.

The King and Bronson were able to gain some distance between themselves and the Trolls. The chanting was sounding more and more distant.

After a while, King Dustin stopped to catch his breath. Bronson, panting, leaned against a big tree.

"The trolls are far behind us now."

Bronson nodded.

"We will cut through the trees." The King paused, scanning the area. "It should not take long to catch up to the others. Are you ready?"

Bronson nodded, although the beaver was still short of breath.

King Dustin said, "The trolls will continue down the open path, away from the others."

"I'll be right behind you," Bronson replied

King Dustin nodded as he rammed his sword into its sheath. The King dashed off the path and into the trees. Bronson followed.

❖ ❖ ❖

When the trolls reached the point in the path where King Dustin and Bronson veered off, the leader stopped.

The leader sniffed the air and glared into the trees as though he could see through them. His eyes gleamed. He then signaled the army of Trolls to follow him into the trees, off the open path.

The trolls continued to chant as they marched through the woods.

DANIEL LEE NICHOLSON

March of the Trolls

We march these woods,
One-hundred strong.
Bellies empty,
But not for long.

To all the beings,
That cross our way,
You will surely,
Die today!

We stamp our claim,
With our big feet.
Then pick their bones,
And eat the meat.

We prowl our grounds,
So, all beware.
You cross our path,
We challenge your dare.

We'll watch you breathe
Your very last breath.
Gouge your eyes,
And stomp you to death!

We are the Trolls,
Mighty and strong,
We're coming for you,
You won't live long.

-15-

Mozart Goes Mad

Mozart's nostrils flared. Smoke thundered out of his nose like an erupting volcano. Mozart's ears vibrated so fast, they hummed. The shepherd dog stood with his feet planted firmly in the ground.

"Get back, Mozart!" Clara exclaimed. The dog did not move back. Clara and Sugar Plum quickly scanned the ground for fallen tree limbs to use as clubs.

Mozart dashed in front of the girls. His mouth looked like a bear trap. The dog took a deep breath and howled. It sounded like a pack of wolves.

"*AAAHUUUUUUUUUUUUUUUUU!*"

A band of five trolls faced Mozart. "You don't scare us." The center troll seemed to be in charge of the pack. He did not appear threatened by Mozart.

Although no more than four feet tall, the troll's shoulders and feet were huge. Hair covered most of its body. The lead troll had a big oblong-shaped nose. A large wart was on the tip.

The lead troll spoke low and deep. Its mouth exposed missing and decaying teeth. The troll faced Mozart. "We like dog meat. If you come without a fuss, we might let one of the girls live."

Mozart shook his head ferociously and stood up on his hind legs.

"*AAAHUUUUUUUUUUUUUUUU!*"

Mozart howled like a changed wolf on the night of a full moon.

The band of trolls nodded at one another, seemingly impressed by Mozart's fierceness. However, none seemed frightened by the shepherd dog.

Clara and Princess Sugar Plum held their clubs higher. Nobody moved. It was a standoff.

Clara inched closer to Mozart. "There's not many of them, and they are half our size."

The group of trolls snarled and pounded their feet heavily. The earth jolted. Small animals nearby scuttled away.

Princess Sugar Plum walked backward without turning around. Nobody seemed to notice. She did not take her eyes off the trolls.

Clara blinked. She hoped the trolls did not notice her chest pounding. The crystal stone in Clara's necklace started changing colors.

The lead troll pointed, hissing at Clara. "We'll take her first."

Then—Mozart attacked the trolls.

It was quick. The dog pinned three of the trolls to the ground before they knew what was happening.

The three trolls squirmed to get free but could not. The other two trolls dodged Mozart and ran toward Clara.

"Run, Clara! You and Sugar Plum, get away," Mozart yelled.

Instead, Clara ran toward Mozart. It did not appear that she saw the two trolls running toward her from the side.

Then the two trolls lunged. Clara was within their grasp. The trolls reached for Clara.

Suddenly—rocks hurled through the air.

A flying rock hit one of the trolls. He fell to his knees, moaning in agony. Blood rushed from the troll's injured nose. The second troll shielded his face and ran into the woods.

Clara turned around. She looked in the direction of the flying rocks and smiled. With a rock in her hand, Princess Sugar Plum smiled back at Clara.

Clara turned back around. Mozart still had two trolls pinned down, but the lead troll had managed to get loose. The lead troll had his big foot aimed at Mozart's head. The troll's eyes were blood-red.

"Mozart!" Clara screamed, running toward the dog.

The lead troll glanced at Clara. His foot was now inches from Mozart.

In less than a blink, Clara leaped through the air. She then turned and kicked the lead troll smack in his nose.

The troll's eyes rolled, and his head vibrated. The creature fell to the ground, holding his face in his palms. Blood covered the troll's hands.

Clara had kicked the lead troll in its nose. The wart on the tip turned purple. Clara watched as the troll rolled around in the grass, holding its nose.

"Clara! Sugar Plum!" King Dustin and Bronson finally reached the girls and Mozart.

"There's King Dustin and Bronson," Princess Sugar Plum said.

Mozart glanced at the King and Bronson. The dog then relaxed his shoulders and released the two trolls. "GO!" Mozart barked, pointing to the trees. Drool dripped from his fangs as he stared at the trolls.

The trolls underestimated the dog once. This time they fled quickly into the woods. Mozart watched until the trolls were out of sight.

"We're glad you caught up," Princess Sugar Plum continued.

Clara and Princess Sugar Plum then told King Dustin and Bronson about their ordeal with the band of trolls.

"Trolls are very dangerous," King Dustin responded. "They attack in packs like wolves. Queen Nordika had warned me about them."

"We didn't see you behind us," Princess Sugar Plum said to her brother and Bronson.

"We were worried," Clara added.

"We went down the open pathway," Bronson replied.

"The open pathway?" Princess Sugar Plum said with raised eyebrows.

"I thought you said that the trolls would go down the open path," Clara said, confused.

"That is right, Clara. I had hoped that the trolls would follow Bronson and me. Then you and Sugar Plum would be safe going through the woods with Mozart."

Both Clara and Princess Sugar Plum gave King Dustin and Bronson a big bear hug.

King Dustin glanced at the thicket of trees behind them. "We better move on. We eluded the large group of trolls for the moment. They may have realized by now that we got off the open path."

King Dustin studied the area around them. "If we go that way, we will still be on course. Mozart, I want you to lead us through the woods."

"Yes, Your Highness," Mozart said with a slight bow.

Princess Sugar Plum scolded her brother, "Promise to let me know the *real* plan next time. You always try to protect me, but I am a Tree Fairy. I can take care of myself."

King Dustin smiled at his sister, "I promise," he said. The King then lowered his head.

Princess Sugar Plum twisted her lip, probably thinking that King Dustin would not keep his word. Everyone knew that King Dustin would always try to protect Princess Sugar Plum and Clara—no matter what.

As they started into the woods, they heard marching and singing from behind. The large group of trolls was catching up to them.

"It's the trolls," King Dustin said. "Let's put some distance between them and us."

"Follow me!" Mozart barked. The others had to run at full speed to keep up with the shepherd dog.

❖ ❖ ❖

The small band of trolls reached the larger group.

The troll in charge of the band spoke to the Commander of the Trolls. "Sir, we followed them to the clearing. We didn't want them to run and hide. So, we didn't approach them." The lead troll gulped and hung his head as he spoke to the Commander.

The Commander stopped marching. He stared at the lead troll with a disgusted look, as though he didn't believe him. Dried-up blood was still clinging to the hair on the lead troll's face.

Then, the Commander was distracted by something in the far distance. His senses were exceptionally sharp. The Commander raised a balled fist to his shoulder, signaling the trolls to hold in place.

"They appear to be headed toward Mount Gruslig," the Commander said.

"Yes, Sir."

"Hmm, it will be dinnertime when they arrive." A wide grin appeared on the Commander's face. He then patted his stomach, "It looks like we'll have *fresh* meat for dinner."

-16-

The Swampland

Deeper in the Black Forest, silence was sometimes louder than noise. The forest was dank, and the trees were still. The ground was soggy and gray. Dead vines—and something else, something crunchy—were mixed in the dirt.

Everyone strode lightly through the muck. A foul odor permeated the air. It smelled like death. Clara walked tip-toe, but it was too late. Her pink dance slippers were already black.

All around, trees and shrubs were covered in moss. The moss hung low like drapery. *Something is out there*, Clara thought. She felt a strange sensation that they were not alone. Her arms prickled with goosebumps as she peered into the trees.

Everybody was quiet. It was as though nobody wanted to disturb the beast that haunted these lands. Other than their footsteps through the mushy terrain, a creepy silence was all that was heard.

Sugar Plum walked alongside Clara. The Fairy Princess's curly hair puffed from the humidity in the air. Princess Sugar Plum lifted her heels off the ground. With her body elevated in the air, Sugar Plum winked at Clara. Princess Sugar Plum's strength was restored. She could fly again.

Clara smiled. She knew that Sugar Plum never gave up hope, even in the most dreadful situations.

Clara tried to lift her heels, but her feet did not leave the ground. She could not fly. Her strength had not been restored. Clara assumed the same about King Dustin since he was not a Tree Fairy either.

Clara shrugged, then glanced back at Bronson. The beaver kept his tail high. Clara noticed that the fur on Bronson's neck was raised. Clara admired Bronson. He never let fear stop him.

"Are you okay, Clara?" King Dustin said with a reassuring smile. The King was walking beside Bronson.

Clara nodded.

King Dustin's shoulders were high, and his eyes looked fierce as he scanned the swampland. The King had not bothered to remove his sword from its sheath.

King Dustin is so brave, Clara thought. Glancing up at the sky, Clara tried to smile. She knew that swords were useless against some of the creatures that lived in the forest.

"Clara," Mozart barked, turning his head slightly around. "I will see anything coming." The dog was still leading them toward Mount Gruslig.

"I know, Mozart," Clara responded, looking around. Mozart didn't know that Clara was looking out for him as much as he was looking out for her. *I won't let anything hurt you, Mozart,* Clara said silently.

"Once we cut through the caves of Mount Gruslig, we will not have far to go to get to Sorceress Serihilda's castle," King Dustin stated.

Clara glanced at the crystal stone in her necklace. It was jet-black as the group continued through the swampland.

❖ ❖ ❖

Krieger, the Ogre, joined Sorceress Serihilda in the courtyard at Zauberin Castle. The Ogre towered above the Sorceress. Krieger became indebted to Serihilda centuries ago when the Sorceress saved the Ogre from being vanquished by a witch of lesser power than herself. Krieger recalled that time, long, long ago:

Centuries ago, Krieger said to Sorceress Serihilda, "I am forever in your debt. I will serve you all of your days."

"I hope you are smarter than your words reflect," Sorceress Serihilda quipped. "I have lived over seven hundred years already."

Krieger responded, "Then I will serve you all the rest of my days."

"Ogre, I only saved you to spite that old witch." Serihilda then flung her black and white hair over her shoulder. "Be gone with you."

"Sorceress, surely you could use an Ogre to help protect your lands ... Uhm ... when you are not around?"

The Sorceress circled the Ogre, looking him up and down. "Have you been in many battles, Ogre?" Serihilda asked.

Krieger smiled with evident pride. "Yes. As one of the oldest and strongest Ogres, I have been in hundreds of battles."

"And have you won most of those battles, Ogre?" Serihilda asked.

"Yes," Krieger replied, with his chest thrust forward.

Serihilda continued circling the Ogre. She nodded, "I see."

Krieger responded, "Then, you will allow me to serve you?"

"Absolutely not," Serihilda snapped.

"But clearly, I have won many battles, Sorceress," Krieger pleaded.

"That is apparent."

"Then I can serve you?" Krieger asked.

A dumbfounded look shone on Sorceress Serihilda's face. Krieger waited for the Sorceress to reply.

"If you have been in many battles ... winning most ... then there is not much fight left in you, Ogre. You are of no use to me."

Krieger hung his head low, his warrior pride diminished. He remained quiet, deep in thought.

After a pause, the Ogre finally responded, "Sorceress Serihilda, my strength is only limited by the extent of your magic."

Serihilda grinned and nodded at the Ogre's remark. "Then you will be quite strong, indeed."

Krieger has served Sorceress Serihilda ever since.

Krieger laughed, recalling that time when he first met Sorceress Serihilda. The Ogre looked around the lush gardens in the courtyard at Zauberin Castle. The grounds were impeccably maintained.

Krieger handed Sorceress Serihilda a hat with a large brim and cotton gloves. "Thank you, Krieger." The Sorceress put them on and then continued to tend her garden.

"Had I followed your advice, I would not know that King Dustin was on his way here, to Zauberin," the Sorceress uttered without looking up.

Krieger chuckled, "Had you followed my advice, King Dustin would not have been alerted that Drosselmeyer's spell had been broken."

Serihilda blew out the side of her mouth, "I guess you are right about that."

"You were supposed to be surveying the area, not using your magic," Krieger remarked.

"I suppose," Serihilda responded.

"Queen Nordika has always protected their realm. The Land of Snow and Land of Sweets have always had a close alliance," Krieger commented.

"King Marc and Queen Arabelle, the monarchs of Konfetenburg, I understand that they were in alliance with Queen Nordika befor–" Serihilda started.

"Yes. But, King Dustin, their son, rules the Kingdom of Konfetenburg, now." Krieger spoke, interrupting the Sorceress.

The Ogre continued, "Because of your little visit to the Land of Snow, Queen Nordika is also aware that Drosselmeyer's spell was broken."

"Krieger, you have told me this a hundred times since I returned."

"They may have only guessed that the spell was lifted, had you not turned the–"

Serihilda interrupted, "I had to."

Krieger responded in a doubtful tone, "You had to?"

Serihilda's eyes glistened. "Well, I could not resist."

"Hmm, but a blizzard in the Spring?" Krieger retorted.

Serihilda did not respond. She continued to tend to her garden. Krieger just shook his head as he walked away.

❖ ❖ ❖

The Commander of the Trolls stopped. He looked at the sky. Vultures were flying above the area of the swampland.

"It appears that those kids tried to find a faster path. They are going through the swamplands." The Commander said, pointing at the vultures in the sky.

"Yes, sir. It appears so."

The Commander sighed, "Argh, I will have to make other dinner plans."

The Commander glared at the lead troll. "Hmm. And whose fault is it that I won't have fresh meat for dinner?" The Commander then licked his lips and patted his belly.

The lead troll quickly walked away.

-17-

The Thing in the Swamp

Mozart heard the eerie swooshing sound first. Then they all heard it. Something was hiding, camouflaged behind the tall grass in the swamp.

Something is in the swamp, Clara thought.

Every time the creature moved, its body slithered and swooshed. Nobody saw it, but nobody needed to see it. The frightening sound let them know that it was headed their way.

Clara and the others dodged behind trees. They used the hanging moss to hide their bodies from the creature.

Water dripped down Clara's head. Her heart pounded. She tried to avoid breathing heavily.

Clara hoped that Princess Sugar Plum was well-hidden. She tried to peek through the wet moss that covered her face. She could not see anything.

The swooshing sound was getting closer. The Swamp Thing was in the middle of the clump of trees where Clara and her friends were hiding.

Clara closed her eyes tight and tried not to breathe. The swooshing sound was passing in front of the tree that she was hidden behind. *Just be still a little longer. It will pass,* she said to herself.

However, it did not pass. The swooshing sound stopped in front of the tree that Clara was hiding behind.

Sniff-sniff

The creature sniffed the air. Clara's eyes went wide, and her heart skipped a beat. Clara pinched herself, trying to be as still as possible.

Clara then heard a rustling sound. It sounded like it was coming from another tree. The creature must have heard it too. The creature moved toward the rustling sound.

Swoosh   Swoosh

Then a rustling sound was heard coming from a different tree.

The swooshing sound of The Thing in the swamp stopped. The creature then moved toward the second tree making the rustling sound.

Swoosh   Swoosh   Swoosh

Then, the rustling sound was heard coming from all around. Clara joined in and started yanking on the moss and branches.

The creature shuffled. It headed in one direction, stopped, and then moved in the opposite direction. It kept moving back and forth, trying to follow the rustling sounds.

Swoosh   Swoosh   Swoosh

Clara peeked. A glint of light caught Clara's attention. With his sword raised, King Dustin charged toward the Swamp Thing.

Clara gasped at the sight of the creature. It looked like a deformed reptile that had turned human, *or vice-versa.*

Just then, Princess Sugar Plum flew out from behind a tree. The Fairy Princess was in front of the monster. She taunted the creature, making faces.

The creature bellowed and bucked at Sugar Plum. Mud flew off its body. It then trudged toward the Fairy Princess.

Not waiting a moment, King Dustin, Bronson, Mozart, and Clara all ran toward Sugar Plum. However, the monster moved faster. Within moments it was inches away from grabbing the Princess. It lunged and thrust its scaly fins at her.

Clara screamed, "It's going to get Princess Sugar Plum!"

The Fairy Princess flew up to avoid being grabbed by the Swamp Thing.

The beast lunged again.

This time, Princess Sugar Plum flew away!

The creature from the swamp bellowed as it chased after Princess Sugar Plum.

Sugar Plum slowed her pace. Apparently, she wanted the creature to follow her.

The Thing in the Swamp followed the Fairy Princess. Its massive body moved swiftly through the terrain of the swampland. It swiped at the tall grass in its path and flailed its fins. It tried to catch Princess Sugar Plum but only caught air.

King Dustin peered into the distance. He then wiped his brow and exhaled. "It cannot fly."

Everyone watched as Princess Sugar Plum led the creature away.

-18-

The Plan

***"There may be more creatures lurking
about."*** King Dustin angled his sword.
"Mozart, let me know if you hear anything
strange."

"I sure will," Mozart barked. The dog
lifted his head and pricked his ears.

"Like that Thing in the Swamp," Clara
added.

Clara turned toward Princess Sugar
Plum. "I was so glad you were able to fly."
Clara lowered her eyes. "I was afraid we
would not get to you in time."

"And don't you ever do that again,"
King Dustin said, speaking to Sugar Plum.

Princess Sugar Plum's eyes jetted from
left to right.

"Sugar Plum?" King Dustin said, wanting confirmation.

"I had to steer it away," Princess Sugar Plum said. "I wasn't sure if my strength had restored enough for me to fly us all away. So, I lured it away."

"But—" King Dustin started.

"You and Clara are still probably not strong enough yet to fly," Princess Sugar Plum said.

King Dustin lifted his palms to the air, giving in. He then hugged his sister.

"You are brave like Queen Nordika," Clara said.

Princess Sugar Plum replied, "Thank you. You are too, Clara."

Clara blushed. She always felt afraid, not brave. Whenever Clara was afraid that her friends were in danger, she would do everything she could to help. *I wish I were brave like Sugar Plum,* Clara thought.

King Dustin's eyes softened as he looked at Clara and Sugar Plum. It was evident that he was proud of both of them.

The group continued to walk in silence.

After some time, Mozart looked over his shoulder, facing the others. "I smell a river ahead."

"I do too," Bronson agreed, sniffing.

"Good. We will rest at the river," King Dustin replied.

"I am hungry. Hopefully, the river has fish," Bronson responded. "The kind we can eat. Nothing big or green," he quickly added.

Clara and Princess Sugar Plum laughed. King Dustin appeared deep in thought as he looked into the horizon.

In the distance, Clouds hung low like still ghosts around the peaks of Mount Gruslig.

❖ ❖ ❖

The river did not show any signs of swamp creatures. It felt quite tranquil in this part of the forest, Clara thought. The lingering aroma of fish being grilled over an open flame filled the air.

Bronson topped the fish with flavorful herbs and wild mushrooms. The beaver hummed a soft tune while he cooked.

Waiting for dinner, Clara and Princess Sugar Plum gathered nuts and fed the nearby animals. The squirrels had brownish-red fur coats with cream on their underside.

"Hello, little squirrel," Clara said to one of the squirrels as she handed it a nut.

"Hello. Thank you for the nuts. We haven't eaten dinner yet," the squirrel responded, waving its fluffy tail.

"We gathered plenty," Clara replied as she and Princess Sugar Plum passed out the nuts.

"Gotcha," Mozart said, playing tag with an otter. The otter did not respond. It did not look happy. It looked like it was trying to protect its territory from the big shepherd dog.

King Dustin did not join the others. He sat quietly on a log and stared at the ripples in the river.

"Dinner's ready," Bronson announced. Everyone joined the beaver by the open flame.

After they finished off the fish, everyone sat huddled around King Dustin.

King Dustin stated, "Queen Nordika's scouts had said that the river would take us directly to the caves of Mount Gruslig."

"It will start to get dark in a couple of hours," Bronson replied, looking up at the sky.

King Dustin nodded, "Yes. We will want to get through the caves before nightfall." The sun was beginning to set.

"The caves will lead to the other side of the mountain. The other side is the Land of Zauberin. That is where Sorceress Serihilda lives."

Clara listened closely. The peaceful sounds of the river were not able to lull thoughts of the mission ahead.

"Tomorrow night, the full moon rises. We have to reach Zauberin Castle by then."

Bronson grunted, and Princess Sugar Plum sighed.

"The full moon gives unfathomable power to the Dark Forces, including the Sorceress," King Dustin stated. "We have to defeat Serihilda before the moon rises. Then we will need to depart the forest as quickly as possible."

Clara nodded with wide eyes.

"At the stroke of the midnight hour, Drosselmeyer will cast a spell. It will prevent the Dark Forces from being able to enter our realm, limiting their power," King Dustin continued.

"So, we need to defeat the Sorceress by tomorrow night," Princess Sugar Plum added.

"Yes. If we do not, the Dark Forces will take over, and all will be doomed in our realm," King Dustin replied. "Let us hope that we do not cross paths with any other creatures, or time will not be on our side."

Bronson grunted, "If we have to cross the river, get through the caves of Mount Gruslig and then journey through the Land of Zauberin to the castle by tomorrow night, then we don't have much time."

King Dustin stood, "You are correct. We must depart now."

Mozart barked.

Princess Sugar Plum said, "I wish my strength was fully restored. Then, I could fly us all, and not just myself."

"Hopefully, we will all have our strengths restored soon."

Sugar Plum nodded.

"We will use those logs to get us across the river." King Dustin pointed to logs piled at the riverbank.

The team rushed toward the logs.

"The Sorceress is very powerful. She is even more powerful than Wizard Herr Drosselmeyer," King Dustin stated. "Queen Nordika was told that the Sorceress could only be destroyed in her human form."

Clara's eyes went wide. *What other form is there?*

When they reached the riverbank, King Dustin said, "We will need two logs. Clara and Mozart will ride with me on a log. Sugar Plum will ride with Bronson on the other."

"I can swim across the river," Bronson said.

King Dustin replied, "I want you to conserve your energy. The current is picking up, so it should not take long to get to Mount Gruslig."

The King sat at the front of the first log. Clara sat behind King Dustin. Mozart sat behind Clara.

Princess Sugar Plum mounted the second log. Bronson then jumped on behind the Fairy Princess.

SPLISH-SPLASH

Off they went, down the river.

"The water is choppy," King Dustin shouted, turning his head slightly.

Clara held on tight to the bark and wrapped her legs around the log as they raced down the river.

The logs rose and dipped with the current. At every dip, the logs went under the water. Clara had to hold her breath to keep from choking.

At times the logs jerked, almost knocking Clara off. She wrapped her arms around the log tightly. Water splashed violently all around them as the logs went downstream. Clara kept her eyes closed.

"Hold on tight, Clara," Mozart barked. Clara nodded as the logs pummeled down the river rapids toward Mount Gruslig.

Halfway down the river, Clara thought she heard singing coming from the mountain. *Am I hearing things?* Clara wondered. She then dismissed the thought.

> **We are the Trolls,**
> **Mighty and strong,**
> **We're coming for you,**
> **You won't live long.**

-19-

Chamber of Horror

The trolls arrived back at the caves of Mount Gruslig later than planned.

Standing outside the cave's entrance, The Commander of the Trolls narrowed his eyes. "What is that floating down the river?" Two objects were headed toward them, bobbing up and down in the water.

"I believe it's your dinner, Sir."

The Commander's eyes glistened. He smiled and nodded his head with relish. "Prepare the fire!"

The Commander and the trolls marched into the cave, chanting.

We stamp our claim,
With our big feet.
Then pick their bones,
And eat the meat.

❖ ❖ ❖

The current was a raging rapid as the logs ripped down the river. The water slashed Clara's face. She kept her head lowered to keep her eyes from stinging.

"We are almost at the shore," King Dustin said. His voice sounded distant as the wind carried his words away.

Clara stared into the back of King Dustin's head. It took her a few moments to process what the King had said.

"This is fun," Mozart barked as he shook the water off his face.

Clara wondered how Mozart was able to maintain his balance, but she dared not turn around. *I'm glad Mozart is okay and not sliding off*, Clara thought as she held on tight, trying to avoid slipping off and being carried downstream to parts unknown.

"Whew!" Within moments, Clara felt the bottom of the river underneath her feet. She was ever so happy to dismount the log.

A brilliant blue glow of light caught everyone's attention. It looked like an undersea grotto, except the mysterious light was coming from inside the cave.

"Everyone, be on alert." King Dustin said, retrieving his sword from its sheath. "We do not know what dangers await us inside the cave."

Clara looked inside the shimmering cavern. *It doesn't appear scary.*

King Dustin continued, "Queen Nordika had said that the tunnels through the Caves of Mount Gruslig would be our best route to avoid detection by the Sorceress."

"Mozart and I should be able to detect any impending dangers," Bronson said, sniffing the air. Mozart pricked his ears and barked.

"Bronson, I want you to hold up the rear," King Dustin stated. Bronson nodded as the group approached the cave.

King Dustin glanced over his shoulder. The King gave an approving nod to Mozart. The dog had positioned himself behind Clara and Princess Sugar Plum.

Entering the cave, Clara was mesmerized by the blue glow. "This place looks magical!" Clara exclaimed.

"Yes. The walls look like they are made of crystal!" Princess Sugar Plum said. The entire chamber shimmered from the ice-blue glow cast by the stones. "Uhm, are the crystals moving?"

"Hmm, they look like they are." Clara glanced at King Dustin. She noticed that the King had put his sword back in its sheath.

"Yes, they are moving," King Dustin said, walking closer toward the wall. Clara and Princess Sugar Plum followed the King with wide eyes.

King Dustin retrieved one of the crystals off the wall and cupped it in his hand. "These are not crystals. They are Glimmer Bugs."

Clara and Princess Sugar Plum gazed at the glowing bug in King Dustin's hand. "Can I touch it?" Clara asked.

"Yes. It won't hurt." King Dustin placed the glimmering bug in Clara's hand.

Clara laughed. The bug's iridescent blue wings tickled her hand as it flew around in her palm.

"It's amazing!" Princess Sugar Plum said.

Mozart scrutinized the glowing bug in Clara's hand, then relaxed.

King Dustin said, "There must be thousands of them." The Glimmer Bugs bounced off the walls in the chamber.

King Dustin glared at a tunnel inside the cave. "I wonder what made the Glimmer Bugs leave the inner chambers of the cave. They typically prefer the deepest and darkest places of a cave."

"Hmm," Bronson replied. The fur on the back of his neck started to rise. "Yes, something made them leave."

King Dustin withdrew his sword, "We will need to stay alert as we proceed."

Clara and Princess Sugar Plum nodded.

Clara gently blew at the bug in her hand. She watched as the bug flew over to the wall. It quickly blended in with the tapestry of Glimmer Bugs lighting the walls.

King Dustin proceeded into the tunnel. "Queen Nordika's scout had said to follow the fragrant scent of flowers. It will lead us through the cave. The Land of Zauberin is rich with beautiful and fragrant flowers. The scout had said that their scent filters through the cave."

Clara sniffed the air but was unable to smell any floral scent. Clara noticed that King Dustin was also sniffing the air.

Looking confused, King Dustin said, "Hmm ... Mozart, I will have you lead us through the caves."

"Yes, sir!" Mozart said. When the dog reached the tunnel, he took a deep breath. "Those aren't flowers that I smell." Mozart proceeded into the tunnel. Everyone followed Mozart.

The glow from the Glimmer Bugs faded as they went deeper inside the tunnel. The winding channel was dark and cramped. They could only proceed single file.

The odor inside the tunnel got worse as they continued. *It definitely doesn't smell like flowers.* Clara held her nose.

After a short while, the horrid smell seemed to overpower everyone except

Mozart and Bronson. To maintain her balance, Clara held onto the walls of the tunnel.

"There's light ahead," Mozart barked. "We must be near the end of the tunnel."

"That's good," Clara coughed.

"I agree," Princess Sugar Plum said.

Once the group made it out of the tunnel, Clara and Princess Sugar Plum drew a deep breath. Clara commented, "It doesn't smell as bad in here." Sugar Plum nodded. Although the air still smelled foul, it was less concentrated.

Clara looked around. The chamber was the size of her parlor at home, she noted. A flickering orange light filtered into the room from an adjoining cavern.

"We'll go through that passageway. I'll take the lead," King Dustin said, pointing to the channel with the flickering light.

As the group proceeded, their shadows followed them. When they got halfway across the room, low, deep grunts echoed off the walls.

Grrr Grrr Grrr

"Did you hear that?" Clara asked, peering around the chamber.

Everyone stood still and looked up. The sound had come from somewhere above their heads.

Mozart growled. The grunting sound then stopped.

King Dustin raised his sword and moved forward. The King signaled the others to stay back.

"Maybe it is just a small animal?" Clara said, glancing at Mozart. The dog's fangs dripped with drool. *Probably not a small animal.* Clara flinched.

After a few steps, King Dustin waved for the others to follow him.

As soon as the group moved forward, the grunting started back up. It was even louder than before, coming from all around the chamber.

GRrrr GRrrr GRrrr

"Look!" Bronson said, pointing. "It's coming from those openings."

King Dustin scanned the space above their heads. The wall gutted out in spots, creating a ledge that wrapped around the entire upper part of the cavern. Holes in the wall or small chambers lined the pathway. The grunting sounds were coming from the chambers in the wall.

GRrrr GRrrr GRrrr

"Wait here!" King Dustin said as he moved toward the ledge.

Clara whispered, "Are those tunnels ... the openings in the wall?"

"They look like it," Princess Sugar Plum said. "They probably connect to chambers throughout the cave."

The tunnels were too short for the average person to walk upright, Clara observed. *But tall enough for a big animal—or creature.*

Clara's mind raced as she watched King Dustin climb up the ledge toward the first tunnel. The grunting sound continued.

GRɪᴛᴛ GRɪᴛᴛ GRɪᴛᴛ

Clara pulled out her crystal stone necklace from underneath her top. *Just in case*, she thought.

The King continued up the ledge. The grunting sound thundered off the walls of the cavern.

GRɪᴛᴛ GRɪᴛᴛ GRɪᴛᴛ

Clara's heart pounded. She tried to peer inside one of the openings. All she saw was darkness. She pointed her crystal stone necklace at one of the openings. The grunting sound did not stop.

GRRRR   GRRRR   GRRRR

Clara shrieked, "They are everywhere!" Beads of sweat dripped down her forehead as she watched King Dustin. The King was almost at the first opening.

Clara pointed at the first opening. "Something moved inside!" Clara exchanged worried glances with Princess Sugar Plum.

Princess Sugar Plum jumped in the air and hovered.

GRRRR! GRRRR! GRRRR!

Clara jerked. Her eyes went wide. A moving shadow from inside the tunnel was about to pounce on the King. "It's going to attack King Dustin!"

Just then, Princess Sugar Plum flew up.

"I'm going, too!" Bronson yelled as he jumped into Sugar Plum's energy field. The beaver was flying by her side.

Clara screamed, "It's about to attack!"

Princess Sugar Plum vaulted toward King Dustin. Her energy force whipped Bronson through the air.

Clara ran toward the ledge. Mozart ran after Clara.

THEN—a blast came from the adjoining chamber.

BOOOOOOOOOOOOOM!

-20-

Cave Creatures

The light was blinding, and the explosion deafening! The blast had come from the adjoining cavern.

King Dustin ran down the ledge. Princess Sugar Plum flew to the ground. Bronson tumbled in the air. Mozart growled. Clara let go of the crystal stone of her necklace.

Silence rang on the chamber's walls. The grunting noise finally stopped.

King Dustin vaulted into the adjourning cavern. His sword glistened, raised for battle. Clara and Princess Sugar Plum ran behind the King. Mozart and Bronson held the rear to prevent another ambush.

A roaring fire raged! The sparks sounded like thunder. The red-orange blaze soared. It illuminated the gray stone walls extending the inferno beyond its mass.

Princess Sugar Plum was right, Clara thought.

Just as in the chamber before, this room also had a wrap-around ledge with small openings on the wall. *Those openings are tunnels,* Clara acknowledged silently. *What kind of creature would create tunnels this deep underground?*

King Dustin shook his head as he surveyed the area. He then directed the others to move away from the chamber's entrance. "Stay close to the wall so that nothing can sneak up behind you."

Once everyone was safely standing against the back wall, the King proceeded further into the cavern, staying clear of the blaze.

Clara squinted her eyes. Pillars of stone extended up from the ground. With the flicks of the flame, it looked like the rocks were moving erratically.

"It smells awful in here," Princess Sugar Plum said.

"... like that narrow tunnel," Clara said.

Looking around, Clara noticed piles of wood, *or something*, around the fire.

A low, rumbling growl startled Clara. Her eyes landed on the beast.

Something is wrong. "What is it, Mozart?"

Mozart charged in front of Clara and Sugar Plum. "Stay behind me!" the dog growled.

Stepping backward, Clara looked over her shoulder.

A menacing shadow was growing up the wall behind Clara. The dark figure was twice the size of Mozart. The beast's head resembled that of a wolf-like animal. Its upper lip jutted out, exposing a mouthful of pointed fangs. Its massive chest was thrust forward, ready to attack.

Clara stared at the shadow of the beast, then quickly turned around. Her pupils then widened. Clara gasped. The shadow on the wall belonged to Mozart.

Clara cast a side glance at Princess Sugar Plum. The Fairy Princess had lifted her heels and was hovering above the floor.

Clara then turned to the other side and looked at Bronson. The beaver's front claws poked through his paws.

Although Clara could not see what the others must have sensed, she pulled out her crystal stone necklace from underneath her shirt.

"Stay back!" King Dustin yelled from across the room.

Clara clenched the crystal stone of her necklace, ready to charge toward the King.

She knew that the others were not going to stay back either.

❖ ❖ ❖

The blazing inferno was still raging in the center of the room. King Dustin made it to the other side of the chamber and shook his head at what he saw in the corner.

"Stay back!" the King yelled. Sensing that the group was about to charge across the floor to join him, he forcefully signaled them to stay back.

The group reluctantly followed the King's orders.

King Dustin turned back around and stepped closer toward the corner. He lowered his eyes for a better view of what was below. A drop of sweat fell from King Dustin's face into a deep dark pit.

King Dustin raised his sword. The light from the fire reflected off the blade, illuminating the area. King Dustin swallowed.

The pit was filled with bones—*thousands of bones.*

"It all makes sense now." King Dustin looked all around the Chamber of Horror as he backed away from the pit.

SUDDENLY, creatures came out from behind the rock formations. The floor shook.

Then more creatures came out from the tunnels in the wall. The chamber was filled with chaos and commotion.

"King Dustin, watch out!" Clara screamed. However, it was too late. One of the creatures stood directly behind King Dustin. It wielded a sharp object at the King.

King Dustin snapped around. He tumbled on rocks but managed to maintain his balance. The King angled his sword at the creature.

Clara and Princess Sugar Plum could have been so focused on King Dustin that they may not have seen the creatures approaching them—until it was too late. The creatures had Clara and Sugar Plum trapped against the back wall.

Mozart and Bronson must have been caught off-guard too. The creatures had them pinned on the ground, holding them down with their large feet. Mozart and Bronson were only able to lift their heads. They looked across the room at King Dustin but were unable to help.

King Dustin stared at the creature in front of him.

"So, we finally meet," the Commander of the Trolls said in a deep voice.

King Dustin did not respond. The King flicked his wrist and gripped his sword tighter.

"I thought I would have to change my dinner plans." The Commander paused, raised his sword, and looked King Dustin up and down. He then rubbed his stomach with his free hand.

"I must admit, I am curious about how you managed to make it out of the swampland." The Commander flashed a smirk. "Although, I am quite pleased you did."

King Dustin looked at his opponent. However, he again remained silent. The King glanced over his shoulder. The pit was only inches away.

"Allow me to introduce myself. My name is Waldemar. I am the Commander of the Trolls."

King Dustin assessed the Commander. Although the top of the Commander's head was just above the King's waist, the Commander did not appear intimidated by King Dustin's size. The King noted that the Commander's eyes were those of a warrior with a surprising glint of intelligence.

King Dustin nodded his head slightly without taking his eyes off the troll. "I am King Dustin Egbert Conrad von Konig of Konfetenburg. Most call me King Dustin."

"Hmm, that may be what they used to call you." The Commander whipped his sword in the air and thrust it at King Dustin's throat.

King Dustin stumbled backward. He felt his heels at the edge of the pit.

The Commander lunged again, ramming his sword. This time, King Dustin shifted to the side.

The Commander pivoted and again thrust his sword at King Dustin's throat. The

King dodged the strike. However, it took him a moment to regain his footing.

The Commander took advantage of that moment and lunged again. It was apparent that the Commander was accustomed to battling opponents taller than himself.

King Dustin shuffled sideways to avoid the strikes. The King awkwardly tried different maneuvers to adjust to the Commander's height. Nevertheless, each time the King slashed his sword, the Commander was able to dodge the strike.

However, with each strike, King Dustin got better. After a few minutes, the Commander and King Dustin were in a fierce battle. The blaze lit the room as clashing metal echoed in the chamber.

Trolls stood on the ledges of the wall like it was a coliseum. They pounded their fists in the air and chanted.

> *We'll watch you breathe*
> *Your very last breath.*
> *Gouge your eyes,*
> *And stomp you to death!*

The Commander seemed energized by the chanting trolls. He started to snarl and grunt as he thrust his blade.

King Dustin was undeterred. He was the best swordsman in all of the Black Forest, and his skills were on full display.

The fire roared, sparks flew, and the trolls shouted with excitement.

As the fight continued, the trolls began stomping their big feet. It sounded like an earthquake.

The Commander and King Dustin fought as if they were the only two people in the room.

The moment was soon broken by rallying cries coming from around the chamber, demanding to be quenched.

We stamp our claim,
With our big feet.
Then pick their bones,
And eat the meat!

"Pick their bones and eat the meat! Pick their bones and eat the meat! Pick their bones and eat the meat!" The trolls pounded their fists in their open hand.

Louder and louder and louder the trolls chanted, **"Pick their bones and eat the meat! Pick their bones and eat the meat! Pick their bones and eat the meat!"**

The Commander then thrust the full force of his body into King Dustin.

King Dustin lost his balance. He gripped his sword as he looked over his shoulder, falling backward.

Clara and Princess Sugar Plum screamed as King Dustin fell—into the pit.

-21-

Land of Zauberin

The fire flared even brighter as if it were declaring victory for the Trolls.

A loud **THUD** resonated from the bottom of the pit.

The trolls stopped stomping and chanting. After a collective gasp echoed throughout the chamber, there was *dead* silence.

Everyone in the cavern watched as King Dustin fell into the pit.

The King's body was soon followed by that of the Commander of the Trolls!

The Commander flailed his arms and legs, trying to prevent the inevitable. However, it was too late. Gravity would win in the end.

All eyes stared at the empty space in the corner of the cavern where the Commander and King Dustin had stood.

Everyone was quiet. It was as though everyone's brain was trying to comprehend what had just happened. King Dustin and the Commander had plunged into the pit.

The Commander of the Trolls must have used too much force when he pushed the King.

The Commander tumbled right behind King Dustin from the force of his own weight. The troll's body fell head first into the pit.

The trolls that had trapped Clara and Princess Sugar Plum let the girls loose and ran toward the pit.

The trolls that pinned down Bronson and Mozart followed the other trolls. All the remaining trolls in the chamber ran.

The ground in the cavern jolted as all the trolls in the chamber ran toward the pit. Their eyes held a look of disbelief.

Within moments, all the trolls surrounded the pit. The trolls closest to the black hole lowered their heads, peering into the black hole.

"NO!" Clara and Princess Sugar Plum shrieked. Mozart and Bronson stood in shock.

A rumbling sound then echoed throughout the cavern as the trolls backed away.

The trolls looked up as they moved away from the hole.

Something was coming out of the pit. The heads of all the trolls followed in sync with the object. Their big noses pointed as the object flew higher and higher. The object then stopped and hovered in the air.

"King Dustin!" Clara yelled.

"He got his strength back!" Princess Sugar Plum exclaimed, watching her brother fly above the pit.

King Dustin had not hit the bottom of the pit. The thud sound had not been from King Dustin's body but rather from the Trolls' Commander.

The trolls stumbled as they ran away from the pit. They hunched their backs and used their arms to protect their heads from the sword-wielding man flying above them.

The trolls trampled the ground as they ran to the ledges lining the walls. They then dodged into the tunnels. The sound of their feet was loud as they ran through the tunnels to other parts of the cave.

Within moments, all the trolls were gone—except the Commander. His body remained at the bottom of the pit.

❖ ❖ ❖

Meanwhile, at Zauberin Castle, the two shadows that lurked in the dungeon appeared restless. With hunched backs, their hoods covered their sunken faces. Underneath the gray cloaks, the frames of their bodies appeared thin, like skeletons.

The dark figures moved slowly around their home in the cell of the castle. First one, then the other, would walk over and peer through the bars of the window. Panting, they paced back and forth across the stone floor.

One never knows the last time the cloaked creatures had been fed. They were indeed agitated and may be very hungry.

❖ ❖ ❖

Having been spared any further incidents, Clara, King Dustin, and the others made it out of the Caves of Mount Gruslig faster than expected.

They were now in the Land of Zauberin. The perfume scent of fragrant flowers engulfed them.

It was nightfall. King Dustin decided that they would sleep and head out at daybreak to Zauberin Castle.

Clara had not noticed before, but she thought the King looked tired. She admired how King Dustin was always able to maintain his focus no matter how tired he was or what perils they encountered. *His parents would have been so proud of him*, Clara thought. *Too bad they never got a chance to see him as King.*

"Tomorrow night will be the full moon. We only have until then to complete our mission." Those were the last words King Dustin said before the group drifted off to sleep.

Darkness gripped the air, choking out the light as they slept.

It was dark when the group awakened. Morning was just beginning to peek through the sky. King Dustin was sharpening the blade of his sword on a rock. Clara wondered if the King had slept at all.

"We must hurry to Zauberin Castle," King Dustin said.

Bronson looked into the distance. "I can see the castle. It will take us several hours to reach it if we continue on foot," Bronson said, pointing.

The King nodded, "That is the only way to avoid detection by the Sorceress." King Dustin pulled at the hem of his jacket. "We must move swiftly."

The group followed King Dustin through the heavily wooded forest.

Clara looked in all directions. *The Land of Zauberin is quite beautiful*, she thought.

Streams and gentle waterfalls provided a background of soothing sounds. Wildflowers and lush foliage scented the air as they proceeded through the land.

Clara had not seen any animals as they walked. *That's odd.* No birds were flying above or rabbits scurrying below. Not even a field mouse squealed.

However, large spotted moths and buzzing bumblebees with stingers were plentiful.

Clara decided to practice flying. She lifted her heels. "Yes, I can fly." Instead of walking, Clara hovered slightly above the ground, flying.

After a short while, Clara thought about her Uncle Drosselmeyer. She cringed, recalling King Dustin's comments about the Sorceress being more powerful than her uncle. She tried to think pleasant thoughts to get her mind off the perils that lay ahead.

"I like flying," Clara said. "It feels like floating inside a bubble." Turning to Princess Sugar Plum, she added, "Thank you for asking the Great Tree to grant me the ability to fly."

"You are most welcome," Princess Sugar Plum said with a wide grin.

"Do you like flying more than dancing?" King Dustin asked.

Without a pause, Clara replied, "Nothing is better than dancing!" Clara then jumped into a grand jete, leaping in the air.

Princess Sugar Plum joined Clara leaping above the ground. The girls danced like butterflies landing on leaves as they leaped gracefully down the path.

Clara and Sugar Plum had endless energy as they danced through the forest. Bronson and Mozart engaged in conversation. However, King Dustin remained silent.

Time seemed to pass quickly as the group headed toward Zauberin Castle.

❖ ❖ ❖

It was very late in the day when the group finally arrived at Zauberin Castle. The sun was beginning to fade.

Clara noticed that King Dustin kept looking up at the sky.

Within an hour, the skies would look like a masterpiece—stroked in shades of purple and ruby red. Then the full moon would begin to rise.

"We have about two hours," King Dustin stated.

"We must defeat the Sorceress before the moon rises. After the moon rises, her magic will become even more powerful. We will never be able to defeat her then."

"At the stroke of the midnight hour, Wizard Herr Drosselmeyer is set to cast his spell. It will prevent the Dark Forces from being able to enter our realm. Our Kingdoms will be spared from the ravages they would inflict upon our lands," King Dustin reminded everyone, adjusting his jacket.

The King summarized, "If we fail to defeat the Sorceress by the full moon, then Wizard Drosselmeyer's spell will likely be canceled by the Sorceress. The Dark Forces will be free to roam our realm."

"And all will be doomed. Wickedness will reign," Princess Sugar Plum said.

King Dustin responded, "That is true." The King gripped his sword. The Sorceress has a servant, an Ogre. We will need to distract him first."

"Once we have the Sorceress isolated, then we will have a chance to defeat her," King Dustin said as he pulled at the hem of his jacket. Everyone nodded.

King Dustin looked at Clara, "I don't know where you fit in the plan. I did not want to involve you. However, Queen Nordika said you might be needed."

Clara said, "I am not sure where I fit either, but I will be by your side, King Dustin." The King nodded.

"Our mission is critical. We must not fail." The King paused before continuing. "It is time to save our realm from Sorceress Serihilda and the Dark Forces!"

"We're ready," Bronson said. The group then marched into the courtyard at Zauberin Castle.

They were ready for battle—*or so they thought.*

The End
of Act Two

"Clara was surprised by the beautiful garden in the courtyard of Zauberin Castle."

ACT 3

-22-

Enchanted Zauberin Castle

Clara was surprised by the beautiful garden in the courtyard of Zauberin Castle. Fragrant flowers were in full bloom, and lush green vines climbed up the walls of the castle.

Clara blinked twice. *Are the vines moving? Are they climbing up the wall?* Clara continued to watch as the vines zig-zagged up the palace walls. Higher and higher, the vines climbed.

Not sure if she saw things, Clara glanced over at Princess Sugar Plum. The Fairy Princess did not appear to notice anything strange with the vines. *Hmm, maybe it was just my imagination.* Not wanting to second-guess herself, Clara looked away.

"Let's walk in the shadows. We will avoid being seen by anyone that may happen to be looking out the windows." King Dustin said, walking alongside tall evergreens that surrounded the perimeter of the courtyard.

An ornate fountain took center stage in the courtyard. Water cascaded down the sides from a gargoyle-like beast centerpiece. Clara gushed at the tranquil sound of the water.

The courtyard seems kind of odd for a Sorceress, Clara thought, glancing around the picturesque grounds. Clara then chuckled, realizing that she had never met a Sorceress. *Maybe this isn't odd at all.*

Bronson glanced at Clara. Reading her facial expression, he said, "Sometimes, beauty isn't as it appears."

Clara gulped and turned around. She stared at the back of King Dustin's head for the rest of the walk through the garden.

Within moments, they made it to the side of the castle. A door leading to the dungeon was unattached. The door had been removed and was upright and resting on its hinges.

"I wonder what happened here?" King Dustin said in a curious tone, lifting the door. The King placed the door on the wall, leaving the entry open after they entered the castle. Muted light filtered into the dungeon.

Clara sniffed. *It smells like dead animals.* She sniffed again. *Or maybe somebody that hasn't taken a bath.* Clara immediately thought of the Ogre.

"There is a staircase ahead," King Dustin said in a low voice. "We must be very quiet when we go upstairs. We will search for the Ogre first."

SUDDENLY, a bumping sound was heard coming from somewhere down the corridor. King Dustin raised a fist, shoulder level, signaling for them to hold in place.

All was quiet—for a moment. After a few moments, they heard the bumping sound again, louder this time.

THUMP! THUMP!

"It's the Ogre." King Dustin said, slightly above a whisper. The King pointed with two fingers. "That way." Everyone glared down the dark corridor that was producing the bumping sounds.

"Bronson, I need you to lead the Ogre out of the castle. Ogres are very strong. Do not confront him."

Bronson nodded.

Mozart looked down the corridor. His eyes were cold. The dog gritted his teeth. Thick drool dripped from his fangs.

Mozart then stretched his neck and shifted his body forward, raising his head ferociously. He looked like he was going to howl—but not a sound came out.

Mozart then charged in front of King Dustin!

King Dustin paused for a moment. Then he vaulted behind Mozart, angling his sword. Bronson lifted his tail and ran behind the King. Princess Sugar Plum and Clara flew behind them.

The smell got stronger as they raced down the corridor. The thumping sound was now bouncing off the walls. The noise banged Clara's eardrums. Her heart pounded.

Mozart is no match against an Ogre. Clara wanted to tell the dog to stop. However, Clara knew it was pointless. She was afraid for Mozart.

Clara held her crystal stone necklace in the palm of her hand and flew as fast as she could. *I have to save Mozart!*

The bumping sound got louder, and the horrid smell was now unbearable. They were close to the end of the corridor.

THUD!

Mozart made it to the end of the corridor and knocked down a door. A piercing howl erupted from the dog.

"No, Mozart!" Clara screamed.

King Dustin tried to stop Mozart, but it was too late. Mozart howled like a beast as he charged into the chamber with the Ogre.

King Dustin wielded his sword and lunged behind Mozart. Bronson was on the King's heels. The beaver's claws extended like talons.

The battle had started.

Princess Sugar Plum looked up. "There's not much space," she said, looking at the low ceiling in the chamber. The space was too tight for her to lift the Ogre with her energy force.

"Magic, please work!" Although unable to see the beast, Clara pointed the crystal stone of her necklace in its direction.

Mozart stood on his hind legs. His massive body blocked the others. Only the Ogre's shadow was seen.

King Dustin charged to Mozart's side. "Get back, Mozart," he shouted.

Mozart growled and lunged. He was ready to attack.

Bronson took a stance on the other side of King Dustin.

Clara jumped to the other side of Mozart, holding her necklace.

Princess Sugar Plum had just enough space to hover above everyone's head.

The battle lines were drawn.

Clara gasped at what she saw in front of them.

It was not the Ogre. Instead, they saw two dreadful-looking figures in gray hooded cloaks. The creatures appeared to have hunched backs.

The creatures slowly removed the hoods on their cloaks. Their fingers were wrinkled with long nails. Long hair draped down their faces.

Nobody moved. All was silent. Everyone stood, paralyzed by the sight of the creatures.

Princess Sugar Plum gasped. King Dustin seemed to choke.

"Dustin? Sugar Plum?" The figures spoke in frail voices.

King Dustin's eyes went wide with shock. Princess Sugar Plum flew down from the ceiling.

"Mother? Father?" King Dustin said with teary eyes. His sword fell to his side.

"Mom! Dad!" Princess Sugar Plum cried.

King Dustin and Princess Sugar Plum ran to the two figures. The two figures held out their feeble arms.

King Marc and Queen Arabelle hugged their children, Dustin, and Sugar Plum.

❖ ❖ ❖

A round of hugs and kisses overflowed in the small chamber. King Marc and Queen Arabelle then communicated how Sorceress Serihilda had captured them years ago.

The King and Queen explained that they had entered the realm of the Dark Forces with a small team of soldiers. Their mission was to retrieve medical herbs that only grew in the lands Deeper in the Black Forest.

They further explained how the Sorceress became aware of their journey and used her dark magic to vanquish all of their soldiers.

"She delighted in having a King and Queen as prisoners, so we were spared." Queen Arabelle said.

King Marc added, "We have been prisoners here, ever since."

"We kept looking out the window in hopes that we might be freed," Queen Arabelle added.

"She is a powerful enchantress," King Marc acknowledged.

❖ ❖ ❖

After the short reunion with their parents, it was decided that Princess Sugar Plum would fly King Marc and Queen Arabelle back to the Land of Sweets.

The others would continue their mission without the Fairy Princess.

King Marc wanted to join his son in battle. However, it was decided that because of his time in captivity, he was too weak.

King Dustin hugged his parents and said goodbye. "I am so glad we finally found you."

"You are very brave, son. I am so proud of you."

Princess Sugar Plum hugged her brother. "I will get them back home safely," she said. She then reached for her parents' hands and flew into the night.

The skies were dark. It would not be long before the full moon rose.

King Dustin, Clara, Bronson, and Mozart headed back toward the staircase. It led to the upper chambers of Zauberin Castle.

Clara held tight to the crystal stone of her necklace and sighed. She had forgotten to ask Queen Arabelle how to use its magical powers.

The crystal stone was jet-black.

-23-

The Beast

The staircase creaked with doom. Light was no longer filtering into the dungeon. Darkness followed King Dustin and Clara with every step.

Like most animals Deep in the Black Forest, Mozart and Bronson could see in the dark. The dungeon glowed like daylight to them.

Clara sensed her heart pounding. She clutched the crystal stone of her necklace until her palms dripped sweat. *Magic, please work.* Clara then let go. The crystal stone plopped against her chest.

"We will need to move quickly and quietly. Is everyone ready?" Holding the door's lever at the top of the staircase, King Dustin glanced back at the others. Bronson was directly behind him on a lower step.

Bronson nodded. He then glanced back at Clara. Clara returned the nod and glanced back at Mozart. Mozart barked.

"Stay behind me," King Dustin said. The King then turned the lever and opened the door. A short passageway led into the Great Hall of Zauberin Castle. Everyone followed single file behind the King.

Clara looked around in awe. The Great Hall was massive, and its furnishings opulent. A grand staircase anchored the room.

As King Dustin, Clara, Bronson, and Mozart moved across the floor, their eyes were drawn up to the tall height of the ceiling.

Suddenly, heavy footsteps broke the silence.

THUMP-THUMP!   THUMP-THUMP!

King Dustin signaled for everyone to stop. The footsteps were coming from behind them.

Clara turned her head around in slow motion. She no longer saw the opulent furnishings. Thoughts of the Ogre filled her mind.

With her head turned around, Clara's eyes rested on the Beast.

"It's the Ogre!" Clara shrieked, stepping backward. The Beast was more frightful than she ever imagined.

The Ogre had been hiding in the shadows—waiting to attack.

"Ahhhhhh-Uhhhhhh!" Mozart jumped up on his hind legs. The dog stretched his neck and howled at the Ogre. Windows in the room rattled.

The Ogre twisted its monstrous face and scowled at Mozart. Its face changed colors in that instant from bone-gray to crimson-red. The Ogre reeked with fury.

The Ogre's legs were as large as tree trunks, and its arms looked like they could take down an army in one strike. The purple and blue veins underneath its skin pulsated like raging rapids about to burst.

The Ogre then opened its mouth. The sound coming out of the Beast could not be described as a scream or a howl.

The Ogre's roar was so mighty that a force of wind followed. Windows in the room shattered. Clara was blown backward, and King Dustin had to hold tight to his sword.

The King charged forward.

Even with his sword raised, the King did not look like a formidable opponent against the giant Beast.

The Ogre raised his powerful leg and then pounded his foot against the floor. The Great Hall shook from the impact.

Bronson ran and stood beside King Dustin. The beaver opened his mouth and extended his front incisors as weapons.

Mozart was closest to the Ogre. He tensed his body until it was as stiff as a corpse. Mozart then flung his torso toward the Beast and vaulted in the air.

"No, Mozart, NOOOOOOOOOO!" Clara screamed.

The Ogre scowled and snorted. Seeing Mozart, the Beast pulled his right arm back like a sling. He pulled it as far as it could go. It looked like it was going to pop out of its socket.

Mozart was in the air and closer to the Ogre. The dog growled as he lunged at the Beast with the full force of his body.

The Ogre then slung his arm. In one powerful motion, the Beast slammed Mozart across the room.

Thump! Mozart's body pummeled hard against a far wall.

Clara gasped.

Mozart's body then slid down the wall and smashed against the floor. ***Thump!***

"Mozart!" Clara screamed.

Clara ran as fast as she could. She forgot that she could fly. When Clara reached the dog, she cradled Mozart's head on her lap. Tears streamed down Clara's face as she looked at Mozart.

Mozart was limp, and his eyes were closed.

"I will make sure he doesn't hurt you again." Clara turned her head and glared at the Beast. She no longer looked afraid. Clara looked like a mother bear facing a predator that had harmed one of her cubs.

King Dustin pointed the tip of his sword toward the ceiling. The King then lifted his body straight up. He hovered in the air, in front of the Beast. The King and the Ogre were face-to-face.

The Ogre stared at King Dustin. The Beast did not blink. He raised his hand at the King. The Ogre's hand was twice the size of King Dustin's head.

The Ogre then thwacked the backside of his hand at the King.

King Dustin dodged the strike. By flying backward, the King was able to avoid being slammed like Mozart.

"Down here!" Bronson yelled, trying to get the Ogre's attention. The beaver then rushed the Beast.

The Ogre narrowed his eyes and looked down. The Beast lifted its strong foot and kicked Bronson squarely in the chest.

Bronson bowled over. The beaver grunted as his body rolled across the floor.

With fierce eyes, King Dustin thrust his sword at the Beast. As he pulled the blade back, red blood dripped down from its tip. King Dustin had pierced the Ogre in the shoulder.

The Beast grunted although the Ogre did not appear to be in pain. His face was now distorted. His veins rippled as he balled up his fingers into fists. One fist after another, the Beast pounded like a boxer.

The King was barely able to dodge the blows.

King Dustin then flew quickly. The King rammed his blade at the Ogre with a powerful strike. Sweat flew off the King's face.

However, this time the Ogre was ready and dodged the assault.

King Dustin and the Ogre continued to battle. Both appeared to have adjusted to the other's fighting style. Neither landed a strike. King Dustin flew, ramming his sword at the Ogre and the Ogre pounded his fists at King Dustin.

On and on, they battled.

After a while, King Dustin was breathing heavily. Although they seemed evenly matched, Dustin could not manage this pace for much longer, especially while flying.

The King glanced out the window at the dark sky. The full moon would be rising soon. The King sighed as if knowing that he had to end the fight soon. They did not have much time left.

While King Dustin had turned his head toward the window, the Ogre shifted his weight.

The Beast raised his fist. The blood in the Ogre's veins was streaming toward his hand. With his huge fist, the Ogre pounded King Dustin in his ribcage.

King Dustin's eyes went wide before closing. The King's body then fell to the floor of the Great Hall.

-24-

Beauty

"King Dustin!" Clara shrieked. She watched helplessly as King Dustin hit the floor of the Great Hall in Zauberin Castle.

Clara looked down at Mozart. "I'll be fine. Go to King Dustin." Mozart was barely able to lift his head as he spoke.

Clara gave Mozart a quick hug, then leaped. This time, she flew across the room.

The Ogre stood above King Dustin. With an intellectual tone, the Beast spoke. "Your arrival was anticipated. The Sorceress has been waiting for you. Although we did not expect additional guests, they are most welcome. As you can ascertain, we are always prepared."

Clara was halfway across the room now. She had heard what the Beast said to King Dustin. *This was a trap.*

"Go back, C-l-a-r-a," King Dustin said in a weak voice. The King was clearly in pain. He tried to lift himself off the floor but could not move.

Bronson was able to move, although very slowly. The beaver hobbled across the floor, trying to get to the King.

Clara flew down next to King Dustin. She choked up, seeing the King in agony.

Clara's body tightened, ready to protect the King at all costs. She craned her neck and faced the Beast. Clara's brown eyes looked black.

The Ogre towered over Clara. "You must be Clara," the Beast said, looking down.

Clara gasped as if surprised that the Ogre knew her name.

"Wizard Drosselmeyer's incantation, a century ago, wreaked havoc on the Black Forest. The Sorceress will have to undo the tragedy. We cannot allow King Dustin to get in the way of her plans."

The Ogre then lowered its arms and curled its fingers. The Beast reached down to grab Clara with its giant hands.

"STOP!" Clara shouted, standing tall.

"You should not have come here. You should have stayed with the others at the lake. The Sorceress was just playing, then."

Clara quickly recalled the tornado at camp.

"I am not going to let you hurt my friends." Clara looked up at the Beast, holding her ground.

The Ogre cocked his head. He stared at Clara as if wondering how she ever thought that she could stop him.

The Beast looked around the room. Mozart, Bronson, and King Dustin were precisely where he left them, barely conscious, on the floor.

The Ogre then stared directly into Clara's eyes. "I have taken down all of your friends, and I will not spare you!"

The Ogre opened his hand and grabbed Clara into his grasp.

Clara closed her eyes. She held the crystal stone of her necklace and pointed it at the Ogre. "Magic, please work!" Clara pleaded.

❖ ❖ ❖

At that moment, Clara's mind raced back to her first journey Deep in the Black Forest. Her thoughts exploded.

Clara recalled that her uncle, Wizard Drosselmeyer, had turned King Dustin into a Nutcracker doll. Drosselmeyer had said that he had given the Nutcracker doll to Clara to hide King Dustin from the evil Mouse King.

Clara remembered her Uncle saying that the Mouse King discovered his plan. Clara recounted how she tried to protect the Nutcracker doll from the Mouse King and his army of mice.

She recalled that King Dustin transformed back to his human form and slew the Mouse King.

❖ ❖ ❖

Clara's thoughts were interrupted by a low swooshing sound. She opened her eyes and gasped. Clara was still in the Ogre's grasp.

The crystal stone of her necklace glowed brilliant black. The light was so bright that Clara had to let go of the stone to shield her eyes.

The crystal stone of the necklace then hovered above Clara's chest.

Clara stared at the Ogre. She could not wriggle free. She watched and waited.

The crystal stone did this before, Clara recalled. Last year, the stone zapped wicked spirits in the form of Lovely Ladies. Clara glanced down, waiting for the stone to zap the Ogre.

Nothing happened.

Clara swallowed as she stared into the eyes of the Beast. *Magic, please work.*

Black piercing light began emanating from the crystal stone. The light swirled in front of Clara and the Ogre. Specks of gold reflected in its radiance.

Clara watched as the glowing light started swirled faster and faster. *The magic is working,* Clara thought. *It is going to zap the Ogre.*

The light swirled and twirled. Within moments, the glowing black light had twisted around the Ogre like a coil.

The Ogre opened his hand, letting go of Clara. The Beast pounded the air and flailed as Clara flew down to the floor, next to King Dustin.

The Beast twisted and squirmed, trying to get loose from the grip of the glowing coil. However, no matter what the Ogre did, it could not set itself free.

The glowing coil emanating from the crystal stone of Clara's necklace had bound the Ogre. The Beast was trapped.

The more the Ogre tried, the tighter the coil wrapped itself around the Beast.

The Ogre's veins pulsated until they burst through his skin. However, even that did not stop the Beast. He continued to twist and turn.

Nevertheless, try as he might, the Ogre could not escape. The Beast was trapped by the enchantment of Clara's crystal stone necklace.

King Dustin managed to stand up beside Clara. The King watched as the coil of light restrained the Beast.

Bronson joined them. Mozart then limped across the floor and stood next to everyone. It was obvious that the dog was still in pain.

Everyone stared at the Ogre.

They all appeared mesmerized by the glowing coil of light that trapped the Beast. Faster and faster, the light swirled. Clara became dizzy, watching.

POOF!

The Ogre then disappeared.

Seconds later, the glowing light streamed back into the crystal stone of Clara's necklace.

Next, a loud **THUD** was heard. The remains, a small remnant of the Ogre, fell to the floor.

Clara gasped. Bronson grunted, and Mozart barked. King Dustin gripped his sword tighter.

"Awe!" Clara exclaimed as she looked at the remains of the Ogre.

Clara smiled, glancing at the crystal stone of her necklace.

The stone was no longer hovering around Clara's neck and had changed back to its normal amber shade.

Then, **IT HAPPENED!**

A fierce wind roared through the Great Hall from the upper chambers.

"It is the Sorceress," King Dustin said. "It's Serihilda!"

Everyone stared in silence.

Piercing purple eyes glowed from the top of the staircase.

-25-

The Transformation

A loud thunderous sound erupted. Flashes of piercing light shot through the darkness like a rocket. Strong gusts of wind whipped through the air. A storm descended upon the Great Hall of Zauberin Castle.

Sorceress Serihilda floated at the top of the staircase. Her green gown lashed the air behind her body. Her long black and white hair raged wildly.

The remaining windows in the room exploded. Shards of glass flew across the Great Hall.

Bronson's thick coat of fur shielded Clara from the missile-like glass. King Dustin was able to dodge the glass, but several pieces of shard struck Mozart. However, the dog's double fur coat protected his skin from being seriously cut.

Although Serihilda's face was hidden, Clara still felt the sting of her purple eyes.

The Sorceress then began to descend the staircase.

Serihilda's hair covered her face like the veil of a widow in mourning. The Sorceress hovered above each step, floating like a ghost. A low humming sound echoed from her body.

Clara put her palms to her ears to deafen the sound.

Watching Serihilda's slow descent to the Great Hall, King Dustin raised his sword. "Everyone, get behind me." The King did not move his head or turn his eyes away from the Sorceress.

Nobody moved. Clara, Mozart, and Bronson remained still. Everyone stood side-by-side, facing the staircase—facing Serihilda.

"Where is my Ogre?" The Sorceress said in an unnatural voice.

Everyone avoided glancing at the Ogre's remnants.

Oh, no. Clara shuddered.

King Dustin responded, "Sorceress Serihilda—"

The clap of thunder and lightning exploded through Zauberin Castle before the King could finish his sentence.

Clara jumped with surprise. Her heart pounded as she stared at Serihilda's face.

The Sorceress had a lovely face with soft cheeks. Her eyes were a brilliant purple shade. Serihilda's hair was both black and white. It flowed down her back, touching the floor.

At first, Clara thought the Sorceress looked beautiful. Then Clara felt something, something eerie. It overtook Serihilda's beauty. Clara remembered what Bronson had said in the courtyard, "Sometimes, beauty isn't as it appears."

Clara felt a sense of horror and evil coming from the Sorceress. It seemed to be as much a part of Serihilda as her lovely face. *She is definitely not as she appeared,* Clara now thought.

"I will ask you one last time," Serihilda paused. "WHERE IS MY OGRE?" the Sorceress bellowed. Her voice echoed throughout the room.

This time, without thinking, Clara stared at the remnants of the Ogre on the floor.

Serihilda's eyes followed Clara's. The Sorceress gasped at the sight of the Ogre's remnants. Serihilda's black and white hair then flew backward as she stared at what was left of Krieger.

"Something is happening!" Clara shrieked, pointing at the Sorceress.

Serihilda's body started vibrating, almost convulsing. The Sorceress was slowly changing, *TRANSFORMING*.

"Clara, stay back," King Dustin said with urgency. The King stepped forward, angling his sword.

Little by little, bit-by-bit, Serihilda began to transform. The Sorceress was changing into something else entirely.

What is happening to her? Clara had a strong sensation to turn away but could not take her eyes off Serihilda. Clara's heart pounded, and bumps prickled her skin as she watched Serihilda transform.

With each step that the Sorceress descended, her shape shifted, and her body contorted.

Serihilda's face changed, too. First, her features became distorted. Her nose and mouth grew, punching through her face, while her cheeks became sunken. Serihilda's lovely face was no longer recognizable. Only the purple color of her eyes remained the same.

"She is turning into some kind of creature!" Clara shielded her eyes and turned away.

"But what?" Bronson replied, looking at the King for a possible answer.

King Dustin did not respond. He stayed focused and ready as he stepped closer toward the Sorceress.

The humming sound got louder as the Sorceress continued down the staircase. Her arms and legs stretched as muscles began forming underneath her skin.

Serihilda's limbs were changing from that of a woman into an animal, possibly even a beast.

Clara gasped when she heard Serihilda's nails push through the skin of the Sorceress. Talons that curled replaced Serihilda's hands. The bone structures continued halfway up Serihilda's arms.

Clara held the crystal stone of her necklace as she stared. Mozart lunged forward, ready to leap. Bronson's rudder tail was high on his back, preparing to strike.

King Dustin stood tall. He held his sword in his right hand and extended his left arm in front of Clara and the others.

Nobody moved. Everyone stared at the Sorceress as she continued to transform.

As Serihilda's body changed, her long hair shriveled up. As the Beast grew, dark gray and black fur started covering its body. Within moments the Sorceress was no less than ten feet tall.

Mozart growled.

"Not yet, Mozart," the King whispered.

With her body transformed, the Sorceress hunched her shoulders. Black and white feathers protruded through her skin, forming gigantic wings.

The Sorceress seemed to grin with pleasure as a tail slithered out from behind. It was as though she was adding jewelry–a final detail.

Clara gasped.

The Sorceress then lifted her head. Her lovely face was no more. Serihilda now had the gruesome face of a vulture. Her scalp was featherless, and her mouth was now a beak that hooked at the tip.

The Sorceress looked like a hideous ten-foot creature–part bird, part beast, *and part something else.*

Clara had to keep her knees from buckling. She opened her mouth, but no words came out. Clara thought with woe, *Serihilda turned into a Sorceress-Beast!*

Clara then glanced down at the Ogre's remnants and hoped that her crystal necklace would do the same on the Sorceress-Beast.

So, it was YOU who did that to my Ogre!

Clara jumped, hearing the Sorceress-Beast in her mind.

"Did you hear that, too?" Bronson said, glancing at Clara.

Clara nodded frantically.

"Me, too," Mozart growled.

"Yes, I heard her, as well," The King confirmed.

The Sorceress-Beast was now speaking, communicating, through her thoughts.

-26-

Full Moon Rising

Part One

Sorceress Serihilda transformed into a Sorceress-Beast. Any likeness to Serihilda was gone—except for her piercing purple eyes.

A gray cloud of smoke emanated from the Beast, suffocating the air in the room.

The Sorceress-Beast flapped its mighty wings, and the smoke was blown out of the broken windows of the Great Hall.

THAT'S BETTER. I CAN SEE YOU NOW.

The Beast continued to communicate to Clara and the others through their minds.

Clara cupped her ears, hoping that it would deafen the thoughts entering her head.

NO SUCH LUCK, the Sorceress-Beast snarled.

Clara gulped, cupping her ears did not work. The Beast was still penetrating their minds with its thoughts.

The eerie thoughts of the Sorceress-Beast continued as it chanted.

FROM LOW, LOOK HIGH,
THEIR FACES TELL THE TALE.
NO SKIN TO PIERCE,
NO BLOOD TO SMEAR.
THOSE NOT ALIVE,
I SUMMON YOU HERE.

FROM LOW, LOOK HIGH,
THEIR FACES TELL THE TALE.
NO SKIN TO PIERCE,
NO BLOOD TO SMEAR.
THOSE NOT ALIVE,
I SUMMON YOU HERE.

FROM LOW, LOOK HIGH,
THEIR FACES TELL THE TALE.
NO SKIN TO PIERCE,
NO BLOOD TO SMEAR.
THOSE NOT ALIVE,
I SUMMON YOU HERE.

Clara swallowed, hearing the chant over and over in her mind. She looked high to the top of the staircase.

"I am not sure what it meant, but be ready," King Dustin shook his head and shifted his weight. He lunged with his sword angled toward the top of the stairs.

Mozart howled. With his sharp ears, the shepherd must have heard them first.

The sound of many feet—*and something else*—echoed from the upper chambers. Clara and the others looked at the top of the staircase. They did not see anything *at first*.

Then, slowly, two-by-two, *they* appeared.

Clara's eyes went wide. Bronson grunted. King Dustin took a deep breath and gripped his sword tighter.

Creatures marched from the upper corridor like soldiers. Their bodies were shaped like a man—but that is where the resemblance ended.

The apparitions had bones that glowed in the dark. They did not have skin, just some sort of see-through filler. The oozy substance was not yellow nor green, but some color in-between.

The skeletal creatures had no eyes, just sockets. An eerie light glowed from the holes in their skull where their eyes should have been.

"What are they?!" Clara shivered, pointing at the phantoms.

The jawbones of the skeletons moved up and down as they chomped on their perfect set of teeth. The unnerving sound sent shivers down Clara's spine.

"Move back, slowly," King Dustin said, extending his arms outward, pushing the others backward.

As the creatures descended the staircase, the green ooze from their bodies dripped, leaving prints on the floors.

"The Sorceress must have conjured up those phantoms," Bronson said, moving backward.

THEY WILL RID ME OF YOU THREE. AND THE OTHER ONE, I WILL PERSONALLY HANDLE FOR SLAYING MY OGRE. The Sorceress-Beast roared into the minds of Clara and the others.

Bronson glanced at Clara with protective eyes.

Standing on his hind legs, Mozart howled with a fierce roar. The remaining glass in the windows broke at the sound. Mozart looked ready to take on the Sorceress-Beast and all the phantoms by himself.

King Dustin stepped forward. "I slew the Ogre," he said.

Clara shook her head and stepped forward. "I-I did that to the Ogre," she said softly.

"Clara, get back!" King Dustin jumped in front of Clara.

The first set of phantoms had now reached the bottom of the staircase. The Sorceress-Beast flapped its wings. It then lifted its body high above the floor of the Great Hall.

The phantoms stopped marching but stood at attention as if waiting for orders.

Clara thrust the crystal stone of her necklace at the Sorceress-Beast. Clara was surprised that the stone's color had not turned black. It remained amber. Clara sighed, not understanding.

YOU SPEAK TOO LATE, KING. I ALREADY READ HER MIND. FURTHERMORE, YOU HAVE OTHER MATTERS THAT YOU SHOULD BE WORRIED ABOUT ... LIKE YOUR DEAR MOM AND DAD.

"You held my parents captive all these years," King Dustin replied, moving toward the Sorceress-Beast.

YES. THAT WAS MY MISTAKE. I SHOULD HAVE JUST DONE AWAY WITH THEM. BUT BE ASSURED, I WILL TAKE CARE OF THEM, TOO.

King Dustin did not respond but continued to proceed toward the Sorceress-Beast.

WHEN I AM DONE WITH ALL OF YOU," the Sorceress-Beast paused in its thoughts before continuing. ***I WILL YANK YOUR PARENTS FROM THE SKY. THEY WILL NEVER MAKE IT BACK TO YOUR KINGDOM ... AND NEITHER WILL YOUR FAIRY SISTER.***

King Dustin grimaced but remained silent. He continued to move forward without lifting his eyes off the Sorceress-Beast.

GO AHEAD AND TRY IT. The Sorceress-Beast said with her thoughts. *DO YOU THINK I CANNOT READ YOUR MIND? IF YOU THINK YOU CAN TAKE ME ON, DO IT.*

King Dustin stopped in his tracks. He shook his head as if he realized that the Sorceress-Beast had read his mind.

The Beast cocked its vulture-like head. *BUT, LADIES FIRST.* It then cast a wicked look at Clara.

King Dustin charged across the floor. Mozart and Bronson followed the King. They each seemed to have forgotten their pain.

Clara then took flight. "I will not let you hurt my friends!" she screamed as she flew toward the Sorceress-Beast.

The Sorceress-Beast flapped its wings.

Clara fell with a thud in front of the Sorceress-Beast.

Clara tried to get up. However, her body seemed to be under an enchantment. She could not move from the seated position.

King Dustin, Bronson, and Mozart gasped, looking at Clara. They paused, only for a moment. The three then rushed toward the Sorceress-Beast.

Part Two

THOSE NOT ALIVE,
BE STILL NO MORE.
THE THREE YOU SEE,
MUST NO LONGER BE.

When the Sorceress-Beast finished the chant, the phantoms charged down the staircase toward King Dustin, Bronson, and Mozart.

Having made it to the center of the Great Hall, King Dustin and Bronson stood ready to fight off the assault by the phantoms.

Mozart did not stop. On his hind legs, he charged the creatures that were closest to him. From the collision, skeleton bones flew in the air as Mozart fell to the floor.

Greenish-yellow ooze covered the shepherd's white coat of fur.

A swarm of phantoms then attacked the shepherd dog. Under the mountain of bones, Mozart could no longer be seen. More and more phantoms continued to pile on top of Mozart.

Clara tried to move, but her body was still under an enchantment. Tears flowed down her cheek as she saw the skeletal creatures overtake Mozart.

The remaining phantoms charged King Dustin and Bronson.

The King wielded his sword and thrust it into the body of one of the phantoms. When the King removed his blade, it was covered in green ooze. However, it did not stop the phantom. The King quickly thought about the Sorceress-Beast's chant, *"NO SKIN TO PIERCE, NO BLOOD TO SMEAR."*

While the King's head was down, a phantom headed toward him. King Dustin looked up just in time. He then flew toward the ceiling, away from the fiend.

As the King looked toward the floor, he saw Bronson about to be attacked by several phantoms. King Dustin then swooped down.

At the same time, Bronson jumped in the air and twisted his body. He then used all his might and slammed the creature in the head with his rudder-like tail.

The phantom's skull flew across the room. A pile of bones fell to the floor, submerged in green ooze. The bones no longer moved.

The King and the beaver exchanged glances. As though they knew what the other was thinking, they smiled as King Dustin used his energy field to lift Bronson off the floor.

One by one, the King and the Beaver attacked the phantoms. King Dustin flew himself and Bronson above each phantom, then Bronson used his tail to slam the skulls off their shoulders.

Within minutes King Dustin and Bronson had taken out all of the phantoms in the Great Hall, except for the pile on top of Mozart.

Rushing to Mozart's rescue, King Dustin stopped in mid-air. Bones and skulls started flying all over the Great Hall. The shepherd dog was maniacal. He was no longer trapped by the creatures. All the skeletal creatures were now loose bones.

Mozart howled as he stood up on his hind legs.

King Dustin and Bronson exchanged curious glances. It was as though they barely recognized the shepherd dog. Mozart stood upright like a wolf in the night. The dog's fur coat glowed an eerie green from the ooze.

To the King and Bronson, Mozart may have looked like one of those wolves that howl in the forest under a full moon.

King Dustin quickly glanced out the window. He sighed in relief. The full moon had not yet risen.

Bronson looked at all the loose bones submerged in green ooze. "No longer be," the beaver chuckled. King Dustin smiled and, Mozart barked.

Part Three

The Sorceress-Beast jerked its head and flew above the staircase of the Great Hall. The Beast looked as though it could not believe what had happened.

As the Beast flew back down to the floor, it flapped its wings. King Dustin, Bronson, and Mozart froze in motion. They could not move. They appeared to be under an enchantment.

However, Clara was no longer under the Beast's enchantment.

Clara choked. She then stood up slowly. Clara repeated as she moved toward the Sorceress-Beast. "I am brave. I am brave. I am brave."

When Clara got close to the staircase, she stopped and stared. The Sorceress-Beast's piercing purple eyes seemed to tear into Clara's soul.

The Sorceress-Beast scowled at Clara. Its purple eyes revolved in their sockets like rolling marbles.

YOU KILLED MY OGRE, AND YOU WILL DIE A TORTUROUS DEATH!

Clara's heart pounded in her chest, but she managed to stand without trembling. She clutched her necklace and said silently, *Magic, please work.* Her necklace still did not change colors. It remained amber. Clara wondered if the magic in the necklace still worked.

I WILL DELIGHT IN TELLING DROSSELMEYER ABOUT YOUR DEMISE. NEVER AGAIN WILL THE POWER OF THE DARK FORCES BE SUPPRESSED!

The thoughts of the Sorceress-Beast rang in Clara's ears. Clara flinched but stood firm. She knew that the full moon would be rising soon. *I don't have much time. Magic, please work,* Clara thought as she clung to her necklace.

The crystal stone still did not change color. It continued to glow bright amber.

THE DARK FORCES WILL TAKE OVER ALL OF THE BLACK FOREST!

Clara avoided eye contact with the Sorceress-Beast as she clenched her necklace in the palm of her hand. Sweat dripped down Clara's forehead. *Magic, please work,* she repeated silently.

DROSSELMEYER AND QUEEN NORDIKA ARE AT THE TOP OF MY LIST. The Beast said through her thoughts. ***IT WILL BE EXTREMELY ENTERTAINING RIDDING THE BLACK FOREST OF THOSE TWO.***

Clara gasped for breath.

The Sorceress-Beast glared at Clara with her rolling purple eyes. ***YOU DIDN'T THINK I'D PERMIT THEM TO LIVE, DID YOU?***

Clara did not respond.

The Sorceress-Beast continued her thoughts. ***I WILL SLAY THEM FIRST.***

Clara's finger trembled as she pointed the crystal stone of her necklace at the Sorceress-Beast. The stone's color still had not changed from amber.

Watching Clara point her necklace like a weapon, Serihilda's purple eyes stopped rolling. "And what do you have there?" The Sorceress-Beast roared.

Clara closed her eyes and gripped her necklace. "Magic, please work!" Clara said in a raised voice.

Clara wondered if the magic of the crystal stone still worked. She wondered if it did, would the crystal stone zap the Sorceress-Beast. She hoped that it would bound Serihilda in a coil of glowing, swirling light like it did the Ogre.

After moments passed, and not hearing anything, Clara opened her eyes.

Clara gawked. The Sorceress-Beast had not been zapped. Nor was it wrapped in a swirling coil of light. Clara looked down at her necklace. The crystal stone was still amber.

Clara then slowly raised her head.

The Sorceress-Beast stood directly in front of Clara now. The Beast hovered over Clara like a vulture about to eat its prey.

"Magic, please work." Clara continued to point the crystal stone at the Sorceress-Beast. Nothing happened.

Clara regretted not remembering to ask Queen Arabelle how the magic of the necklace worked. She continued to repeat under her breath. "Magic, please work."

Still, nothing happened. Clara lowered her sad eyes. *Sorceress Serihilda is even more powerful than the magic in my necklace.*

Clara glanced back out the window. Clara knew that within minutes, the moon would be rising. *We are out of time.*

Clara did not know it—*but she was also out of time.*

Suddenly, the Sorceress-Beast spread its massive wings. Within a blink of an eye, it moved toward Clara.

King Dustin, Bronson, and Mozart watched powerlessly. They were still frozen in motion. They could not stop the Beast.

Clara was still holding onto her necklace's crystal stone when the Sorceress-Beast engulfed her in its mighty wings.

Seconds later—Clara was gone.

Tears rolled down King Dustin's face. Mozart whimpered, and Bronson grunted in agony. They watched as the Sorceress-Beast ruffled its feathers. A smug look seemed to appear on the Beast's face.

The Beast's wings then began to change colors. Within moments the wings of the Sorceress-Beast were purple, matching its eyes.

Next, an over-powering lavender scent filled the Great Hall. Purple dust floated in the air from underneath the Beast's wings.

King Dustin's teary eyes followed the dust as it flew higher and higher toward the ceiling.

Bronson lowered his head as though he could not watch.

Tears streamed down Mozart's muzzle as the shepherd dog mourned for his beloved Clara.

An eerie screeching sound then erupted from the Sorceress-Beast. The purple dust coming out of its body was now black.

The wings of the Sorceress-Beast also changed from purple to black.

Moments later, smoke gusted out from underneath the wings of the Beast.

King Dustin's face went pale as he watched the end of Clara. *This was all my fault.* The King then closed his eyes.

The Sorceress-Beast cringed and twisted. The Beast seemed to moan.

King Dustin opened his eyes.

The Sorceress-Beast seemed to be writhing in pain.

Slowly, the Sorceress-Beast began opening its wings. It continued to moan as though it was in agony.

When its wings were fully opened, out stepped Clara, clutching the crystal stone of her necklace.

The light emanating from the crystal stone shone like sunshine. The glow cast a sphere of light around Clara. The powerful amber glow surrounded Clara's body like a bubble.

Clara then stepped out of the smokey wings of the Sorceress-Beast. Looking at the crystal stone of her necklace, she pointed it at the Sorceress-Beast.

Clara closed her eyes. In deep thought, she lowered her head as though she was making a wish. Clara then opened her eyes.

Clara stared at the Sorceress-Beast. She then watched as the Beast vanquished into black dust.

King Dustin, Mozart, and Bronson looked on with amazement.

Next, a sudden gust of wind blew into the Great Hall. The wind swirled and twirled. It lifted the black dust higher into the air and blew it out the broken windows.

The Sorceress-Beast was gone.

Clara sniffed as a strong scent of lavender filled the air in the Great Hall.

It took them a moment to notice, but King Dustin, Bronson, and Mozart were released when the Sorceress-Beast turned to dust. The Beast's spell over them was broken. The King and his friends were no longer frozen in motion.

Realizing they were free of the enchantment, King Dustin rushed over to Clara. Mozart leaped, and Bronson ran.

"Are you okay, Clara?" King Dustin said, checking Clara from head to toe.

Mozart barked before Clara could respond. "I thought you were gone." The dog then jumped up and licked Clara all over her face.

Clara laughed.

"I am fine," Clara said gleefully. She was so glad to have such great friends that cared so deeply for her.

Clara glanced down at her necklace. "The crystal stone formed a bubble around me. It protected me from the magic of the Sorceress-Beast. I didn't feel anything."

King Dustin smiled with relief. He, along with Bronson and Mozart, gave Clara a bear hug.

Clara hugged them back before continuing. "I believe the necklace did not change to the color black or use its magic earlier to keep its power a secret from the Sorceress-Beast."

Bronson nodded, "That makes sense, Clara. The Sorceress-Beast would have felt magic coming from the necklace."

"Yes," Clara responded.

The King then turned and glanced out the window. "The moon," King Dustin said in an anxious tone.

Clara exclaimed, "Did it already rise?! Were we too late?!"

King Dustin, Bronson, and Mozart ran over toward the window facing the courtyard. Clara chose to fly.

Glowing from the light, they all looked into the horizon just as the full moon began to rise.

King Dustin and Clara smiled, realizing that they had achieved their mission.

Bronson patted Mozart on the back. "Whew! It was close."

The friends looked out the window for a while. Nobody said a word. The moon took center stage, glowing brightly in the black, velvet sky.

Then, without fanfare, an explosion of streaming meteors showered the sky. Everyone gasped with delight.

"It is time that we head back to our realm," King Dustin finally said.

"Queen Nordika and Wizard Herr Drosselmeyer will be waiting for us," Bronson added.

"King Marc, Queen Arabelle, and Princess Sugar Plum, as well." Clara smiled.

"Is everyone ready to fly back?" King Dustin asked, ready to leap out the window.

Clara looked around anxiously. "Oh, wait."

Clara then flew across the room and landed on the floor next to the remnant of the Ogre. She picked up what was left of the giant beast and joined the others at the window.

"It might not be a good idea to leave this here," Clara said, lifting the remnant of the Ogre.

Everyone nodded in agreement.

King Dustin then looked directly at Clara and said, "Clara, now you can talk with animals."

Clara nodded with a smile.

The King continued, "Now you can fly."

Again, Clara nodded.

King Dustin then looked at Clara's crystal stone necklace. "And now you have the magic of an Enchantress."

Clara's face flushed as she glanced down at her magical necklace.

King Dustin then proclaimed, "Clara, you are now one of us! You have become a part of our realm, Deep in the Black Forest."

-27-

Grand Finale

The halls of the Ice Palace in the Land of Snow burst with excitement. Everyone was in a state of frenzy. Servants collided in the corridors while bustling back and forth in preparation for the celebration.

It had only been two days since Clara, King Dustin, and the others had returned from the Land of Zauberin. They saved all the kingdoms Deep in the Black Forest by vanquishing Sorceress Serihilda.

Wizard Herr Drosselmeyer was then able to cast a spell on the Dark Forces, preventing them from entering the other realm in the Black Forest. The other kingdoms were, once again, protected from the wickedness of the Dark Forces.

A huge celebration was planned. Queen Nordika had less than forty-eight hours to organize the event. The occasion was also in honor of King Marc and Queen Arabelle's rescue and returned to the Land of Sweets.

All the dignitaries, people, and animals from all the nearby lands and kingdoms would be in attendance.

❖ ❖ ❖

"That ball gown looks beautiful on you, Clara!" Princess Sugar Plum exclaimed. Clara and Princess Sugar Plum were in one of the Ice Palace's upper chambers, getting dressed for the celebration.

Clara beamed as she looked in the mirror. She was wearing a pure-white, floor-length gown trimmed with delicate lace. A long sheer tulle cape complemented the dress. The hooded cape was decorated with shimmering crystals. White fur was attached to the hood. The train on the cape extended several feet, trailing the floor.

"This is the most beautiful gown I have ever seen!" Clara glowed as she twirled around. She lifted the train of the cape and said, "Thank you so much, Princess Sugar Plum. I will return it in pristine condition."

"It is yours to keep," Princess Sugar Plum said. "Today is a special occasion. I want you to have the gown as a keepsake of the events."

Clara glanced at her shoes. She was wearing glimmering gold satin dance slippers.

"You must have the slippers, too. They go with the gown!" Sugar Plum exclaimed.

"Thank you so much! You are the sister I never had," Clara said with sincerity. She then gave Sugar Plum a big hug. Clara always wanted to have a sister.

"And you are a sister to me, as well, Clara." The girls danced and twirled gracefully around the room. Both looked like they were floating in the air. And they probably were.

❖ ❖ ❖

The evening sky in the Land of Snow shone in abstract strokes of pink and purple. Snow no longer covered the land. The enchantment was broken.

The Ice Palace looked magnificent, with a prism of lively colors reflecting off its windows. It was as though the castle dressed for the occasion.

The orchestra was robust. The instruments could be heard well beyond the walls of the Ice Palace. Guests started arriving early in the evening. The Sound of Music serenaded them upon their arrival.

Ladies arrived in colorful gowns of the finest silks, chiffons, and satins. Men, escorting the ladies, marched in formal soldier attire or vibrant shirts and black pants.

The fur of the animals in attendance shone like mink. Their claws glistened like porcelain.

Many of the people and animals wore crowns and carried scepters.

After being greeted, Guests were ushered to a buffet in the main dining hall. A feast of every sort of food delicacy had been prepared for the event.

Each time the dining hall doors opened, the sweet aroma of buttery cookies and flaky pastries scented the air.

Roasted lamb, dumplings with smoked pork, whipped mashed potatoes, sweet peas, and spicy red cabbage awaited everyone.

A chocolate cake of several layers with creamy white frosting was topped with sweet cherries. The cake was set on a table in the middle of the room. Guests lined up for a slice.

After feasting, attendants ushered everyone to their seats in the Great Hall for the main event.

❖ ❖ ❖

Inside the Great Hall of the Ice Palace, Lieutenants from Queen Nordika's army formed two rows. Silver medallions hung around their necks. Each shepherd dog looked regal and bold, maintaining erect shoulders and ears.

The two rows of shepherd dogs stood opposite each other. Their bodies created a center aisle for the processional. Pink rose petals, gently dropped, served as a pathway down the aisle.

Vases of white jasmine flowers were everywhere in the Great Hall. The abundance of flowers smelled like a botanic garden.

Silk ribbons of gold with bundles of white baby's breath blossoms draped the walls. A stage of high-back gold velvet chairs and a center throne, bedazzled with crystals and gems, were in the front of the room.

At precisely eight o'clock, *trumpets blared!* It sounded like a thousand elephants. Everyone in the Great Hall stood and turned to face the entry doors. The Main Event was about to begin.

A hum of respect filtered the room as The General processed down the center aisle. The shepherd's eyes and ears canvassed the room as he marched. The General was always on duty.

When The General was halfway down the aisle, all eyes turned to the entry doors. "Oohs and Aahs," erupted.

Escorted by her uncle, Wizard Herr Drosselmeyer, Clara looked radiant. The crystals in her white ball gown shimmered. It appeared as though Clara was walking on a cloud as the soft cape trailed behind her.

When Clara made it down the aisle, she gracefully stepped on stage and walked to her place. She waved and smiled before taking her seat. Clara was careful to pull her cape around. It fell over her shoulder and dropped to the floor.

Once Clara was seated, Oohs and Aahs, erupted again. King Dustin and Princess Sugar Plum stood at the entry doors.

King Dustin, dressed in his formal court attire, completed his attire with a heavy gold crown. His blue and red uniform was adorned with gold cords and brass buttons.

Princess Sugar Plum wore a sparkling tiara that complemented her pink chiffon gown. The Princess wore her red curly hair in a high bun. Soft tendrils framed her face. Sugar Plum's brown skin glistened under the light.

Tonight, for this prestigious occasion, most guests would call Princess Sugar Plum by her formal name, *Princess Leyna.*

After King Dustin and Princess Sugar Plum reached their places on stage, the orchestra switched selections and played the *March of Konfetenburg.*

The room exploded with applause. Guests welcomed back King Marc and Queen Arabelle with tears of joy in their eyes.

The Monarchs of the Kingdom of Konfetenburg exuded confidence and poise. They marched down the center aisle dressed in full court regalia from head to toe. Gleaming crowns adorned their heads.

The King and Queen proceeded with the ease of someone that had done it many, many times before.

King Marc and Queen Arabelle smiled at their children, King Dustin and Princess Sugar Plum, as they took their places on the stage.

The music stopped, and the lights dimmed.

As quiet as a whisper, the sounds of a harp, flute, and violin streamed through the Hall. The music started softly but soon became more intense.

At the same time, a single crystal beam of light lit the center aisle. The guests gasped with anticipation.

Queen Nordika, the Snow Queen, stood in the spotlight. With the grace of a prima ballerina, she stepped onto the center aisle of rose petals.

The Snow Queen looked ever so lovely. She wore a white flowing silk gown. A crown of gentle white flowers adorned her long hair. Her blue eyes greeted her guests.

As the Queen proceeded down the center aisle, each pair of shepherd dogs bowed like clockwork when she reached them.

Although graceful and elegant, Queen Nordika exuded the confidence of a warrior. The guests wore bright eyes and broad smiles as they watched the Snow Queen process down the aisle. All was quiet, no Oohs, nor Aahs. When the Queen reached the stage, she took her place on the throne.

King Marc then stood. He glanced over his shoulder and requested that King Dustin join him. King Dustin stood, then joined his father.

"Son, I could not be prouder. You have carried out the duties as King with courage and compassion."

King Dustin humbly lowered his eyes.

King Marc continued, "Without your stepping up as Ruler, there may not have been a Kingdom left for your mother and me to return to."

King Marc patted his son on the shoulder with immense pride and appreciation.

"As I am still alive, your title will revert back to Prince. However, there will come a time when you will again wear the crown as *King of Konfetenburg.*"

King Dustin looked at his father as though saying he could wait for that day. It was evident that the boy King was overjoyed that his mother and father were back home.

King Marc continued, "At that time, the Kingdom of Konfetenburg will be fortunate to have you as its Ruler, once again." Queen Arabelle then joined her husband and son at the center of the stage.

"Everyone, please join us in showing our deepest appreciation to Prince Dustin Egbert Conrad von Konig of Konfetenburg."

The King and Queen of Konfetenburg hugged their son. All guests then stood in thunderous applause. Princess Sugar Plum joined her family and hugged her brother, Prince Dustin.

The special moment continued for a while. After several minutes, the King, Queen, Prince, and Princess of the Land of Sweets, Kingdom of Konfetenburg, returned to their seats on stage.

Queen Nordika then stood. The Great Hall went silent as she spoke.

"Bravery is not demonstrated through actions completed by a courageous person. Bravery can only be demonstrated by someone who acts in spite of their fears. That is the true essence of bravery—to act in spite of your fears.

"Clara, you have once again demonstrated true bravery. Because of your bravery, you defeated the most powerful and evil enchantress, Sorceress Serihilda. In doing so, all the people and lands Deep in the Black Forest were saved from her wickedness."

Queen Nordika then stepped across the stage. The Queen stopped once she reached Clara. With warmth and appreciation, the Queen smiled and lifted the palm of her hand, signaling Clara to rise.

Clara's knees trembled as she rose from her chair. She immediately curtsied. Queen Nordika kissed Clara on both cheeks.

In a firm voice, Queen Nordika announced:

"I proclaim that on this day, Clara Stahlbaum is now *Princess Clara of the Land of Snow!*"

It seemed to take Clara a moment to grasp what the Queen had said. Although the crowd was loud with applause, standing on their feet, Clara did not seem to notice. When Clara finally processed what Queen Nordika had said, her face flushed.

Mozart then joined the others on stage. Secured to his back was a satin pillow holding a gleaming tiara of crystals. Queen Nordika retrieved the crown and gently placed the tiara on the crown of Clara's head.

Tears flowed down Clara's cheeks.

"Princess Clara, you are charged with the great honor and duty to assist me in protecting the people, animals, and creatures that live Deep in the Black Forest."

Suddenly—the lights brightened, and the orchestra began to play.

Clara stood tall and hugged Queen Nordika, accepting her duties as ***Princess of the Land of Snow***.

❖ ❖ ❖

After the pomp and circumstance ended, the audience quieted. A single light illuminated the Great Hall, landing on Princess Sugar Plum.

The Fairy Princess stepped to the center of the floor.

A current of electricity seemed to be coming from Sugar Plum. The spark started in her fingertips as she began to dance.

The spark continued to the crown of her head, electrifying her tiara of sparkling crystals, sapphires, and emeralds. Sugar Plum's fingers then began to move rhythmically like waves in the sea.

"Spectacular," Clara whispered, amazed by Sugar Plum's artistry.

Princess Sugar Plum turned and twirled, dancing a circle of pique turns. She then quickened her step and danced double, and then triple pique turns across the floor.

Not an eye blinked as they watched Princess Sugar Plum move her arms from one graceful position to another like a swan taking flight.

The audience collectively gasped as Princess Sugar Plum masterfully performed Tombe-Pas de Bourree, Glissade, and Saut de Chat.

The dance was a beautiful piece that seemed to depict a young girl that triumphed.

Prince Dustin then walked over to Clara and extended his hand. "Princess Clara, may I have the honor of this dance?"

Princess Clara blushed. "Yes, Prince Dustin," she said softly, accepting Prince Dustin's hand. "I have to get used to being called *Princess Clara.*"

Both laughed as they waltzed across the floor.

After the selection ended, all the guests crowded around to congratulate the newest Princess Deep in the Black Forest, ***Princess Clara of the Land of Snow.***

-28-

Adventures Deep in the
Black Forest

The walls of Clara's bedroom shimmered. It
was high noon, and rays from the sun
glistened like gold.

    Clara and Mozart returned home,
unnoticed, in the quiet of the night. Clara laid
in her bed. Mozart was asleep on the floor.
One of his paws covered his eyes from the
rays of the sun.

    Clara thought about all that had
happened since the start of summer camp at
Lache Lake. She thought about the frogs and
laughed.

    Clara's thoughts were immediately
interrupted by fast-approaching footsteps.

The footsteps were followed by a loud **THUMP**, waking Mozart.

Fritz barged into Clara's bedroom, slamming the door against the wall.

"**Ruff-Ruff!**" Mozart barked as he woke.

Fritz petted the dog with a wide smile.

"When did you get back?" Fritz asked, not bothering to look up at Clara.

Before Clara could answer, Fritz continued, "Mom and Dad are still away on some medical mission."

"Good boy, Mozart," Fritz said, continuing to pet the dog.

"**Ruff-Ruff!**"

"Uhm—" Clara started.

Fritz interrupted, "Where did you find, Mozart? He was gone when I got back from camp." Fritz petted Mozart behind the ears. "Mr. Godfrey said he was lost."

"Hmm, Uncle Herr Drosselmeyer brought me back last night. He told me to tell everyone hello," Clara said, avoiding Fritz's question.

"Where did you go, boy?" Fritz did not appear to be listening to Clara. He continued to rub Mozart behind the ears. "I posted signs everywhere for you."

"You did?" Clara said, surprised. "Uh, on the way home, we found Mozart wandering around Kunkel Street. Poor thing." Clara reached down and patted Mozart on his head.

Mozart barked, "That was quick thinking." Fritz only heard the dog bark. He could not understand or speak with animals, like Clara.

"Everyone was worried. After that weird tornado at camp, they did a roll call. Nobody could find you," Fritz said.

"Uhm–"

"Uncle Drosselmeyer sent a message to the Camp Counselors. He said that he had picked you up to help out in his village," Fritz continued.

Clara looked down. "Yes, I was needed to help the cottage people that had taken ill near his old mill."

Fritz nodded. "When I got back home, Mozart was gone, too. Hmm." Fritz glared at Clara as if he were deciphering clues.

Clara chuckled. "Mozart was probably hanging out with a brave prince saving lands Deep in the Black Forest from an evil Sorceress." *Nobody would believe the truth, anyway.*

"Here you go again." Fritz shook his head. "Last time, it was a giant mouse. Now, an evil Sorceress. You make up some of the best stories."

Clara smiled, winking at Mozart.

Fritz glanced at Clara's rocking chair. "What's that?"

Clara gulped. *I knew I should have put that away.* "Uhm, just a costume for a dance performance. Miss Patti ordered gowns and tiaras for all the girls."

By the time Clara finished her sentence, Fritz had already lost interest and was walking toward the door. "I'm spending the weekend at Bruno's."

Mozart barked, getting Clara's attention.

"Uh, I almost forgot," Clara said. "Uncle Drosselmeyer wanted me to give you something." Clara reached underneath her bed.

"You have something for me?" Fritz asked.

"Yes. Uncle Drosselmeyer made this for you," Clara said, handing the object to Fritz.

Fritz's face lit up. "What is it?" He asked, staring at the peculiar toy.

"It is an Ogre Nutcracker," Clara said.

"This is the best!" Fritz said with wide eyes. "He looks mean and fierce."

"Yes, very mean," Clara replied. Mozart barked in agreement.

"I cannot wait to show Bruno!" Fritz said. He then bolted out of Clara's room.

"You were right," Mozart barked. "Fritz was the best person to keep the remnant of the Ogre."

Clara nodded. She then lifted the crystal stone of her necklace. "I still do not know how its magic works."

Mozart pricked his ears.

Clara continued, "When I faced the Ogre at Zauberin Castle, thoughts flashed through my mind."

"What kind of thoughts?" Mozart barked.

"I was thinking about Christmas Eve when my Uncle Drosselmeyer gave me the Nutcracker Prince doll." Clara paused.

Mozart cocked his head.

"Somehow, the necklace knew my thoughts," Clara said.

"So, it was reading your mind," Mozart said.

Clara tilted her head and twisted her lip. "I think so. Maybe that is how the magic works. Somehow, it knows my thoughts and acts on them."

Mozart nodded his head.

Clara continued, "The crystal stone *must* have read my mind. That is when it turned the Ogre into a Nutcracker doll."

"That makes sense."

"And when the Sorceress trapped me in her wings, I saw purple dust," Clara said.

"That must be why it turned the Sorceress into dust," Mozart barked.

"Yes! That must be how the magic works. The crystal stone reads my thoughts."

"But, I wonder how it knew to hide its magic from the Sorceress-Beast?" Mozart said.

"Hmm, I guess I still have a lot to learn about how its magic works," Clara said.

Suddenly—a burst of light glowed from the crystal stone. It lit up Clara's face like a lantern. Clara beamed, looking down at her enchanted necklace.

❖ ❖ ❖

That evening, Clara stood at her bedroom window. White clouds of smoke streamed out of the nearby chimneys. Except for a stray cat, the streets were empty.

Clara had changed into an emerald green dress with matching pantaloons. Although the crystal stone from her necklace glowed amber gold, it could not match the sparkle coming from the crystals in Clara's tiara.

Clara glanced at Mozart and said, "I told Mrs. Koch that we would be spending the weekend at Marie's."

Clara scanned the room to be sure that she did not forget anything.

"Yes, Princess Clara." Mozart bowed.

"Before we left, Prince Dustin had said that he, Sugar Plum, and Bronson would wait for us at the Ice Palace." Clara secured her tiara as she spoke. "Are you ready?"

Mozart nodded. His eyes gleamed with anticipation.

"Then we are off to our next adventure!" With Mozart by her side, Princess Clara flew out of her bedroom window.

Soon, Princess Clara and Mozart would join Prince Dustin, Princess Sugar Plum, and Bronson on one of many more adventures Deep in the Black Forest.

The End

And the Beginning of:
The Adventures of Prince Dustin and Clara

PRAISE FOR
PRINCE DUSTIN AND CLARA

<u>Prince Dustin and Clara: Legends of the Black Forest</u> (Book Three)

"This enchanting story does not tell a binary tale, only pitting one villain against one protagonist. No, instead, there are several intriguing characters with whom to loath or become enamored."
—TYD Foundation, Fort Worth, Texas

"The lush, luminous colors and imagery of the cover art draws you into a soaring enchanted journey. There are perilous twists and turns through mysterious magical settings, with vivid descriptions of nature, creatures, and surprising moments of humor. I wanted to know what happens next after each page!"
— Rachel Brunn, Member of the Performing and Visual Arts Communities, San Francisco

<u>Prince Dustin and Clara: Secrets of the Black Forest</u> (Book Two)

"Makes me feel nostalgic for my time having lived in Germany. It's always a treat to find a book that includes German words and names with fantasy elements from the Nutcracker. I also quite enjoyed reading the many descriptive passages by Nicholson."
—Log Cabin Library

"The Nutcracker with renewed life. It is given new life up with secrets, monsters and creatures, dark wizards, and the strangest forest in the world; tied with unexpected twists and turns of a magical bow; and turned into an epic fantasy of bigger and better proportions. In other words, do not miss this series."
—Kids Lit Review

"The author brilliantly explores themes of magic, adventure, the struggle against evil, and destiny."
—Readers' Favorite

"Highly recommended for young fantasy enthusiasts who look for strong female protagonists, fantastic encounters, and a can-do attitude that prevails."
— Midwest Book Review | Donovan's Bookshelf

"What a magical tale it is! ... It offers quite a bit of adventure and unexpected twists and turns the entire way through. While it does have its sweet and magical moments, it carries just as many sinister ones. There's a bit of mystery thrown in and a wonderful sense of urgency. "
—Bookworm for Kids

"An epic adventure that once you start reading, you can't put down. I loved everything about the story, from the magical kingdoms to the brave characters and even the really scary creatures."
—Reader Views Kids

"The author did an amazing job hooking the reader in the story to keep them reading more. I like the fantasy elements, such as the animals could talk."
—LitPick

"Prince Dustin seeks out Clara for her help, and they soon begin a dangerous journey through the deepest and darkest part of the Black Forest where they come face to face with magical and monstrous creatures."
—Kids Bookshelf

Prince Dustin and Clara: Deep in the Black Forest (Book One)

"The Nutcracker and the Mouse-King, gets a reboot, one that's full of action and adventure and a little magic too ... In fact, there are many female characters in this novel, such as Sugar Plum and Queen Nordika, who are strong role models for all readers."
—Dance Advantage

"You know a book is going to be good when you can't walk by it without picking it up."
—Mom Does Reviews

"A compelling premise ..."
—School Library Journal

"Even the way the dancers were described gave me a hint of nostalgia for the classics. This is truly an exceptional book, one that made me long for my childhood and wish that I had had this book to read to myself every night."
—Readers' Favorite

"Especially fans of The Nutcracker are going to want to grab this one and get lost in Clara's tale. Since this is the first book in the series, there's a promise of more to come—and I can't wait to see where the story goes from here.
—Bookworm for Kids

"Lots of action ..."
—Fit Ballet

"An exciting fantasy adventure based on the fairy tale, The Nutcracker, young readers will enjoy."
—Kids Bookshelf

Thank You!

We would like to thank all the reviewers for taking the time to read and write a review of *Prince Dustin and Clara*.

Danielle Wigfall
Publicist
Fossil Mountain Publishing

Discussion & Notes

Audiences around the world have enjoyed *The Nutcracker* ballet ever since its premiere in St. Petersburgh, Russia, in 1892. The ballet is based on a retelling by Alexandre Dumas of E. T. A. Hoffmann's classic tale, *The Nutcracker and the Mouse King*. The ballet was originally choreographed by Marius Petipa and Lev Ivanov with a score by Pyotr Ilyich Tchaikovsky. It continues to be a holiday favorite around the world.

In our retelling of *The Nutcracker*, the **Black Forest** was chosen as the setting for the book series because of its proximity to the location in Dumas' adaptation and likely the inspiration for the "Snow Scene" in the ballet. In addition to being rich in history and culture, the Black Forest has many legends, myths, and folklore making it an alluring place for an enchantment—*or magical setting for a fairy tale.*

The first installment in the series *Prince Dustin and Clara*, "Deep in the Black Forest," retells the story of *The Nutcracker* ballet with a re-imagining of the Snow Scene. The thrills and surprises continue in Book Two, "Secrets of the Black Forest." Book Three, "Legends of the Black Forest," concludes the series as Prince Dustin and Clara travel even deeper into the forest on a perilous mission.

Nicholson chose German names for the characters, animals, and places based on the word's general meaning or definition. One exception is the name of Clara's dance teacher in the book, *Miss Patti*. That name was chosen in homage to Daniel Lee Nicholson's first ballet instructor in Chicago. A fun activity for children is to look up the German words for their English equivalents. The German word, *Zauberin*, was a hint of what was to come in Chapter One.

Our books are family-oriented and were written to appeal to readers of all ages. Nicholson strives to transport readers to magical lands far, far away, once upon a time. To appeal to all ages, Nicholson aims to write scary scenes that are viewed differently by readers through each reader's unique lens. For example, the *Lovely Ladies* in Book Two were probably envisioned differently by 10-year-olds than their older siblings. And probably nobody envisioned what they actually looked like from Nicholson's perspective. *Whew!*

Be sure to tell your family and friends about **Prince Dustin and Clara** as they travel to realms Deep in the Black Forest. **The Adventures of Prince Dustin and Clara** coming soon!

"There is no limit to what a person can do that has been inspired by The Arts!"

– Fossil Mountain Publishing

About Us

Author
Daniel Lee Nicholson was born and raised in the Midwest. He has been a performer and ambassador of the performing and visual arts ever since his first performance as a soldier in *The Nutcracker* in Chicago. Nicholson performed in various productions of *The Nutcracker* ballet spanning 10 years. He currently resides with his wife in the Los Angeles area and works in the Media and Entertainment industry.

Publisher
The mission of **Fossil Mountain Publishing LLC** is to captivate and entertain; engage and inspire young readers and readers of all ages by publishing family-oriented books that promote reading and literature; technology and *The Arts*. We strive to develop applications and to incorporate technology into our platforms so that our readers can fully immerse themselves in great stories.

– Visit us at www.FossilMountainPublishing.com

CPSIA information can be obtained
at www.ICGtesting.com
Printed in the USA
LVHW091435190921
698212LV00005B/89